the living treasures of Japan 人間国宝

Interviews and text by Barbara Adachi   Photographs by Peccinotti   Drawings by Michael Foreman

Foreword by Jo Okada

Introduction by Bernard Leach OM

Edited and designed by Derek Birdsall

人
間
国
宝

the living treasures of Japan

Kodansha International Ltd.   Tokyo, New York & San Francisco

Published by Kodansha International Ltd.,
2–12–21 Otowa, Bunkyo-ku, Tokyo 112 and
Kodansha International/USA, Ltd.,
10 East 53rd Street, New York, New York 10022
and 44 Montgomery Street, San Francisco, California 94104.
Copyright 1973 by Omnific.
Art Director and Designer: Derek Birdsall AGI FSIA
Art Editor: Martin Causer
All rights reserved.
Printed in England by Westerham Press.

LCC 73–80959
ISBN 0–87011–204–X
JBC 0070–784081–2361

The Tradition of Hearts and Hands

Japanese handcrafts are known throughout the world for their great variety and high quality as well as for the long history of each craft.

This book, which portrays some "Living National Treasures" – the masters of traditional Japanese handcrafts – and their works, from a new angle, was commissioned by Mobil to describe the traditional crafts as they exist in modern Japan. As one of those consulted from the start of the project, I would like to congratulate the management of Mobil Sekiyu and to say something about this book.

As far as I know, Japan is the only country that has legislation to preserve traditional crafts by designating "Living National Treasures" or, to be more precise, "holders of Intangible Cultural Properties." The Cultural Properties Protection Law is unique in that it applies not only to tangible cultural properties like fine classic paintings and sculptures but also to invisible ones like techniques and skills of performing arts and crafts. As these techniques cannot exist without human beings embodying them, the law designates such persons as objects of protection. For instance, when a certain type of potter's technique is selected as an Intangible Cultural Property, the honor goes to a potter who has mastered the technique to a high degree, rather than to the technique itself. Sometimes a whole group is designated as a holder of an Intangible Cultural Property.

Since the enactment of the law in 1950, altogether thirty-seven persons (in thirty-one types of craft) and seven groups (for seven types) in the field of handcraft have been given the honored designations. The Japanese government's Cultural Agency actively sponsors training courses for prospective successors and regular exhibitions to help the public understand traditional crafts and to encourage craftsmen to develop their skills; the leading role at these functions is played by the Living National Treasures. Government stipends are granted to them annually to help improve their techniques and train their successors.

In introducing these Living National Treasures, Barbara Adachi conveys, as noted by Bernard Leach, accurate pictures of the craftsmen and their techniques. These, together with the superb photographs by Harri Peccinotti and drawings by Michael Foreman, which form an integral part of the text, give us images of the living treasures as never previously seen in other books.

Mrs. Adachi interviewed all these craftsmen and artists, watched them at work, learned of the difficulties involved in their crafts, and most important of all, reached their hearts. Hers is not a mere technical commentary or a simple introduction; what she achieves here is a warm portrayal of the truly creative processes through which the raw materials regarded with so much tenderness by these master craftsmen are made into things for everyday use. Mrs. Adachi, herself a lover of traditional crafts, establishes heart-to-heart communication with the Living National Treasures; she grasps the tenderness they feel for materials, their concern for those who will use the objects, and their pursuit of beauty – the workings of their hearts vital to their crafts.

As I noted at the beginning, Japanese handcrafts are varied, and each has a long history. Japanese craftsmen created many designs and improved techniques to meet the requirements of each era; but it is their hearts and responsive hands that have maintained the long traditions of their crafts. The heart and hand are symbolic and typical of things Japanese; seen in this light, this book has succeeded in sensitively presenting the essence of things Japanese.

In concluding, I pay tribute to the generous cooperation of the officials of the Cultural Agency as well as of the Living National Treasures, which made the preparation of this fine book possible.

Jo Okada
Director
The National Museum of Modern Art, Tokyo

The Unspoken Language of Craftsmen

This book, written around the lives of some fourteen selected craftsmen who have been designated Living National Treasures by a national cultural committee and the Ministry of Education, is the best I have come across dealing in the main with contemporary traditional Japanese crafts. Instituted in Japan, this singling out of individuals as holders of important skills in traditional arts and crafts is as far as I know unique and appropriate, because no nation has loved things of beauty in daily life as much as the Japanese. The average reader may not be aware that most artists and craftsmen of Japan over the centuries owe their depth of insight to Zen Buddhism. This may also be seen in *Chado*, the way of life called Tea, which was originally the aesthetic relaxation of monks, as also the Noh cult of drama.

Barbara Adachi gives clear, well-written descriptions of inherited techniques developed round each variety of raw material, in the making of textiles, lacquerware, paper, woodwork, stencils, pottery, swords, etc. Not only are these techniques made vivid, but also the important good relationship of artisans and younger apprentices with their masters is beautifully enhanced by quoted conversations. The spontaneous respect of the craftsman for his master can be likened to that of a good conductor with his orchestra : the one ensures good music, the other good crafts. Behind the master craftsman may be imagined the kind or stern Zen master guaranteeing the creation of truthful beauty.

The travelling visitor is always struck by the quiet orderliness of Japanese workshops and may wonder how this is achieved. Good workshops are dependent upon inner discipline. A parallel existed under the medieval craft guilds in Europe. Behind these guilds, at the height of Christianity during the first half of the eleventh century, more development evolved than in any preceding five hundred years, as Kenneth Clark helped us to rediscover in his recent television lectures on European civilisation. In the building of Chartres, the aspiring Gothic arch and the flying buttress were used, resulting in the splendid great glass window illustrating unified Faith and adoration.

Similarly, in the sixth century Buddhism arrived in Japan from Korea, China, and distant India and was brought to a crest under the wise and gentle leadership of the Regent Prince Shotoku. The crafts flowered. Many of the old craftsmen quoted by the author refer back to the Nara and Heian periods of spiritually-centred culture that raised Japan to a medieval stage of evolution.

With the development of scientific knowledge in the West, intellectualism became predominant. The humble beauty of hand-crafts vanished and the artisan was replaced by ranks of artist-craftsmen. In searching for a wider validity today it is important to realize this because the best artist-craftsman becomes aware that his own work can rarely rival such purity as may be found in earlier times of simple Faith. Nevertheless, at his truest he is capable of something beyond, that is the use of knowledge as the faithful servant of intuition or even inspiration. In the Buddhist aesthetic of Soetsu Yanagi, artist and artisan sit without rivalry at the topless, bottomless, round table of his Kingdom of Beauty.

Of the craftsmen chosen for this book, I write mainly of those I know, the foremost of whom is Shoji Hamada. This chapter is the most perceptive and well-written description of him both as artist and man I have yet seen. My reason for placing him first is not so much for his fame, but because he stands fairly and squarely between traditional and individual craftsmen. He is a truly round man — not only in person but in personality. I have never known anyone so balanced between head, heart, and hand. He occupies a unique position between peasant art and pure artistry, insofar as he has achieved something new in Japanese art. In avoiding egotism he always learned from the simple craftsmen. A widely travelled man of culture, Hamada is at home in the East as well as the West. He cannot help knowing that he knows, but his admiration has always been for what he calls the "unconscious creativity" of the folk.

The world of folk art is coming to its end because the sap on which it depends is drying up. The future, therefore, lies in the hands of the artist-craftsmen. The late Soetsu Yanagi, philosopher and leader of the folkcraft movement in Japan, standing before the facade of Chartres with Hamada and myself in 1929, said of the West, "You need a new gospel" — by which he meant that which will enable anyman to produce true work for everyman once again.

All through the chapters of this book the generous response from the craftsmen to the perspicacity of Barbara Adachi's questions is noticeable. One recognizes on both sides an eagerness for exchange of principles and practice. Her warm and accurate description of the materials employed in the making of *kozo* and *gampi* papers I can corroborate. I have known Eishiro Abe since 1935 and still use his lovely papers for painting and drawing. He lives and works at Yakumo, near Matsue, one of only two villages in all Japan still retaining the purity of this craft. Good hand-made papers were made in Japan as early as A.D. 756 and are preserved in the Imperial treasure house, the Shoso-in. They even later found their way to Europe and were used by Rembrandt and other artists for sketches and etchings. The vanishing of such beautiful paper today, when there is an obvious market amongst artists and craftsmen the world over, is a serious cultural loss.

Tatsuaki Kuroda is another of my friends. I bought a tray made by him as far back as 1911. Associated with the Japanese Folk-craft Society, he was trained by his father as a lacquerer and is a fine craftsman, rightly regarded as an artist. As a Living National Treasure, his work has inevitably become expensive. I cannot have paid more than a pound or two for that tray, but the black lacquer *natsume* (tea caddy) inlaid with mother-of-pearl, which he recently gave me, is valued at hundreds of pounds.

Amongst the woods Kuroda especially loves is a variety called *keyaki*. This resembles English figured oak, which asserts its twisting character under the sharp tooth of a plane. We read that it takes fourteen coatings of transparent lacquer to temper this tendency. Raw lacquer, like poison ivy, affects the skin of some people quite seriously. Although almost immune, I got blisters between my fingers the first time I used it.

Kuroda has a strange and unusual appearance, as if lacquer had entered his bloodstream. His face reminds me of a portrait of an actor by that fine woodblock artist Sharaku, about two hundred years ago. The recognizable peculiarity found in some of his work is possibly due to his own born nature and deserves special credit.

The inclusion of a great swordsmith of today is of special significance in Japan. The soul of the samurai was likened to the blade of a sword separating truth from falsity, as life from death. Made by the highest skill of craftsmanship, the sword was the sharp edge of power. Its form and material are superb. Mrs. Adachi's description of the workshop of Akihira Miyairi, at Takaki, about 110 miles north-west of Tokyo, vividly gives every detail in the forging of a blade.

Happiness is in the wrinkles of the face of Ayano Chiba, who looks back on a long lifetime of devoted hard work in the two-thousand-year-old tradition of hemp spinning, weaving, and indigo dyeing. This is a delightful portrait of a hitherto little-known craftswoman, who has been given this honour through the excellence of her work.

In this volume many chapters are devoted to city crafts, such as the one on Heiro Kitagawa dealing with the traditional silk weaving for the very best costumes and produced by this house from ancient to modern times. Again the reference of standards goes back to the Nara and Heian periods. The crafts of a capital differ from those of the countryside as the cultivated from the wild rose, as a prince's costume from a peasant's. It is not competition. Who can say which is best? The refined may be over-refined, country-ware may be rough, but more downright.

This is a time for bridge building between apparent opposites. The north-west seaboards of Europe and the north-east seaboards of Asia are the geographical polarities of culture. Whether by sea or air the serious traveller is made aware of this fact. Isolation is at an end: we need to stretch ourselves, each to understand the other, so that the future may be global and fulfilled.

This book is an attempt to introduce the real spirit of Japanese crafts to the Western mind. Nothing less than the criteria of truth and beauty applicable or understandable to both East and West are sufficient.

Bernard Leach

安部榮四郎

In A.D. 610, in the capital of Nara, Prince Shotoku Taishi is said to have watched a Korean priest make paper from the crushed fibers of hemp. The prince allegedly remarked that a more durable and less brittle type of paper could probably be produced from the bark of *kozo* (paper mulberry; *Broussonetia papyrifera*). The great Buddhist regent, whose cultural enthusiasms are legendary, is credited with inducing farmers to cultivate thousands of paper mulberry plants. He also urged Japanese craftsmen to master and perfect the imported paper-making techniques, for he had correctly assessed the increasing need for paper in an era of cultural progress and religious fervor that placed great importance on the copying of Buddhist sutras.

Today, in a small mountain village in Shimane Prefecture on the Japan Sea, some three hundred kilometers southwest of Nara, Eishiro Abe makes *washi* (traditional "Japanese paper") using the ancient technique of suspending mulberry fibers in water and draining them on a fine screen to form sheets of paper. The invention of the suspension method is attributed to a first-century Chinese statesman, Ts'ai Lun, but it was the Nara craftsmen who perfected it. The Japanese refinement of the water suspension technique included the softening of the fibers by boiling and the addition of a mucilaginous vegetable material to the pulp and water mixture. The sticky vegetable starch (*neri*), made from the root of the *tororo aoi* (a tuber similar to taro), allows the *kozo* fibers to float uniformly on the water and to adhere evenly to the screen on which they are caught, thus producing a thin sheet of paper. Using this traditional method, known as the *nagashi-zuki* technique, seventy-one-year-old Abe works daily over his wooden vats to produce Izumo paper, named after the district in which he lives, the area associated with the creation myths of Japan. "My family has been making paper for generations," the white-haired craftsman remarked. "This whole area has engaged in the craft for well over three hundred years, probably over a thousand years, although we have no written records. We do know that paper making developed greatly in the eighth and ninth centuries, and provincial paper makers were producing fine *kozo* and *gampi* (*Wickstroemia canescens*, a thyme shrub) papers. *Mitsumata* (*Edgeworthia papyrifera*) was not widely used until the Edo period. Today, I use *kozo*, *gampi*, and *mitsumata* to produce sixty varieties of handmade paper that I always keep in stock and about one hundred other types that I make in smaller quantities or on special request."

Piles of *washi* filled two large tatami rooms in the back of Abe's rambling house in the hamlet of Yakumo. In one pile of his stock papers there were four types of pure white and one of a heavy, flat blue-black; another pile included eighteen shades of natural or beige. Still another was composed of various browns and grays, four yellows, and four greens, as well as six blues ranging from a pale foggy tone to indigo. Interspersed were eight hues of reddish pink.

Among the colors he himself has recently developed, Abe includes a lively willow green, deep violet, and crimson. Large sheets, all measuring about one meter by sixty centimeters, of midnight blue, iris purple, buttercup, pine green, and cranberry, lay in orderly piles. One tall stack consisted exclusively of natural unbleached papers in various textures, some with salt-and-pepper scatterings of bark particles, others with flakes of bark the size of a thumbnail, wisps of colored fibers or tiny squares of colored paper scattered at random just under the surface. Some papers felt silky, others were porous and filmy. Some sheets were stiff, glossy, and thick, others were dense and flat, limp and fibrous, coarse or bumpy. The variety of textures was enticing to the touch and the range of colors heady.

"Paper must be natural to be beautiful," Abe said, his earnest frown accentuated by his black eyebrows. The word *shizen* ("natural") punctuates his conversations, for he tries to reproduce only natural colors and uses vegetable dyes almost exclusively – indigo plants, safflower, lily root, tree barks. He also uses other natural products such as soot or mineral pigments.

Most of the colors used for the *washi* Abe makes today can be found in the eighth century papers preserved in the Shoso-in. "One of the greatest privileges of my life was the chance to study some of those beautiful papers still stored in the Imperial Repository in Nara," he remarked. "There I saw religious scrolls, examples of calligraphy, and many types of stationery of hemp, *kozo*, and *gampi*. Their colorful dyes include various shades of yellow, pink, red, blue, brown, and green. Some are decorated with painted or brush-stencilled designs, others are made of fibers of two or three colors in one sheet, a technique taken up and refined in the Heian era. Although we know some of the hemp paper was imported from China, the Shoso-in papers tell us how highly developed was the art of paper making in Japan by 756."

A great spur to the paper industry was provided by the Empress Shotoku's order in 770 that a printed paper charm be inserted in each of the one million miniature wooden pagodas she commissioned for distribution throughout the land. Religious enthusiasm soon made the copying of Buddhist scriptures an important industry, and paper production was increased to supply clerics and courtiers, bureaucrats and priests. In the Heian period that followed, sutra copying proceeded at an even more frenetic pace, and the devout often hired scribes to assure an accumulation of sufficient merit to enter Buddhist paradise. Official documents increased in number and paper makers throughout Japan were kept busy supplying official needs, but it was the aristocrats who, by making letter writing an art in itself, gave paper an important cultural role. In the aesthetic atmosphere of Kyoto, the reputation of courtiers and noblemen rose and fell with the skill they displayed in the art of correspondence. A lovelorn lady receiving a "next morning letter" from the titled gentleman who had left her bed just before the light of dawn judged his protestations of delight not only by his poetic imagery but also by the color and texture of the paper he chose, the way he folded it, his brushstrokes, the significance of the blossom attached to the note, and the demeanor of the messenger who brought the missive. As Lady Murasaki's *Tale of Genji* and Sei Shonagon's *Pillow Book* tell us, the rule of taste governed all Heian life, especially affecting the choice of clothing, letters, and gifts. The worth of ministerial petitions, letters to the emperor or empress, and the poems that made up the fabric of everyday communication of the "people who counted" in the imperial capital owed much to the paper on which they were written; and paper as a gift was in a class with silk.

In the four centuries that followed, the types of paper produced increased, as did its uses, and by the Edo period, paper was no longer a luxury. Sliding house partitions (*fusuma*) of paper, often decorated, became an outstanding feature of Japanese architecture. Translucent sliding windows (*shoji*) let light into castles and shops while providing privacy. Paper had many ritual uses: folded, as Shinto prayers of purification, held in the mouth during the formal examination of a sword to prevent defilement of the blade by one's breath, and used by guests at a tea ceremony as a container for sweets. Matrons and courtesans traditionally stifled their sobs with the tissues carried in packets in the folds of their kimonos. Even the erotic connotations of paper were illustrated in the popular prints of love scenes of the "spring picture" variety. Scroll paintings and screens by great artists were more often done on paper than silk. Even during the long period of seclusion that Japan endured under the Tokugawa shogunate, paper similar to that used for woodblock prints found its way to European studios, where Rembrandt and other artists esteemed it of excellent quality for sketches and etchings. Beautifully illustrated and bound hand-printed books of the Edo period have survived natural disasters, the unique quality of the paper insuring that, even after dousings of water and subsequent drying, the pages do not stick together. Paper was commonly used for clothing by all classes, since it provides warmth and is remarkably waterproof. Paper linings often remain in good condition after the fabric of a garment has disintegrated.

The Izumo paper that Abe makes today is sought after particularly for decorative sliding panels, which for centuries have offered architects and designers a creative medium. The abstract quality of the blue and white squares on the *fusuma* in the most famous seventeenth century tea ceremony room at Kyoto's Katsura Imperial Villa was rediscovered by Japanese and foreign artists, including Bruno Taut, Kenzo Tange, and Walter Gropius in the twentieth century, inspiring imaginative use of paper as an architectural material in contemporary houses of both Japanese and Western style. In a country where letter writing is still an important skill, handmade *washi* is considered essential for all important correspondence as well as for calligraphy and poetry. Manuscripts and testimonials, commendations and important speeches are still brush written on fine papers whose textures add a unique quality of elegance. Among those who use paper made by Abe are print artist Shiko Munakata, stencil artist Keisuke Serizawa, potters Bernard Leach and Shoji Hamada, as did the late Nobel Prize-winning novelist, Yasunari Kawabata.

The fact that *kozo*, *mitsumata*, and *gampi* papers are durable and resistant to water and heat has endeared them to artist and archivist alike. The tough sinewy bark of the *kozo* makes a very strong paper characterized as masculine and stern. *Mitsumata* fibers produce a smooth, fine textured paper noted for its feminine elegance. The rare *gampi*, a type of wild thyme, yields the noblest paper of all, distinguished by an elegant gloss and hardness not unlike vellum.

Abe explained that most handmade *washi* is made of *kozo*, since the paper mulberry can easily be cultivated. "*Kozo* paper is good for woodblock prints and sliding doors. If *kozo* is likened to linen, *mitsumata* resembles cotton because it wears well and therefore is appropriate for book bindings and visiting cards, and *gampi* is like silk, the aristocrat of the three. *Gampi* is soft to the touch but lustrous and smooth and makes dignified letter paper of top quality. To make many of my papers, I mix two types of pulp. All sorts of textures and surfaces are possible by varying the mixture and the grain of the pulp."

Leaving the beautiful, heavily beamed farmhouse in which he lives surrounded by Munakata paintings, Hamada teabowls, Kawai pots, a veritable museum of ancient paper products and a large collection of folk art objects, Abe led the way outside. "It is such a beautiful day," he

exulted. "We are so lucky to have a glorious day like this during the rainy season!" He gazed happily over the adjoining fields where rice and vegetables had recently been planted in small patches of ground between the surrounding hillocks. A large flock of sparrows twittered noisily in a grove of bamboo; other bird songs combined to create a choral background. Abe spoke softly with the pleasant drawl characteristic of the Izumo dialect. In a small field behind his house, twenty drying boards were propped casually against simple racks, each board papered with three or four sheets of *washi*.

"This is already dry," Abe said. "See how my hands slip smoothly over it. On a dry day like this, drying takes just over an hour." He lifted the closely textured heavy paper, which clung hard to the bleached boards, and pulled it sharply to peel it off the board with a loud snap. The grain of the pine wood on which the *mitsumata* paper had been drying was visible on one side of the paper, the other side was delicately patterned with a watermark of the screen on which it had been made. "I must work fast because the paper has to be removed as soon as it is perfectly dry. Overdrying hurts the fibers," he explained. After stacking the drying boards neatly in a shed, he strolled through his compound of storehouses, where bunches of dry *kozo* hung from the eaves. *Kozo* resembles rice straw, but since *washi* is never made from the rice plant, the term rice paper is a misnomer. Across the narrow road that climbs through the village, drying boards were propped in front of several thatched cottages.

In front of a modern Japanese country house, two women sat on the ground cleaning wet strips of bark. "These women do a troublesome job so meticulously," said Abe after a cheery exchange of greetings. The *mitsumata* branches are cut in the mountains and bundled for steaming in a huge cauldron. The softened bark is then peeled off in long strips, which are hung in the sun to dry. Once dried, the strips of bark are placed in a fast-flowing stream to be softened and naturally bleached by the clear, cold water before the bark is scraped to remove the black outside. It is the inside, or white, bark that is used to make paper.

Women working on the long, sticky strips of white bark slide their small scythelike blades up the strips; their fingers work so fast at picking out bits of black that the blemishes and specks of bark seem to appear from nowhere. The cleaned fibers are then stacked and ready for a twenty-four-hour soaking in a barrel of water and subsequent rinsing followed by boiling in huge, wood-fired kettles, with rice-straw ash lye or soda ash added as a softener and bleach. Final rinsing in a long trough of pure water precedes another removal of blemishes. *Kozo* and *gampi* bark is processed in the same way as *mitsumata*, with some occasional variations in the sequence or the timing.

Another group of pink-cheeked country women work by the side of the road near a shed in which the white bark is cooked with lye in two great kettles. The women, seated on boxes, rinse the cooked strips of white bark in a trough of running water and then shake the strips and, chatting to each other all the time, scratch, pick and splash at them to remove the tiny grains of dark bark that still adhere. "But this is cold work in the winter. This is fresh well water, you know."

In the earthen-floored workshop, several men worked at troughs of water. Balls of pulp about the size of soccer balls filled earthenware dye pots and blue plastic buckets. Some of the bast was pure white, but much of it was the slightly yellow natural color that Abe prefers to use. A small wooden mortar with a lever-operated mallet is used to beat the pulp. At one end of the workshop an electric beater was chewing noisily; it is good enough for many papers, but hand-beating is essential for special textures and most *gampi* paper. Dyeing usually precedes beating. A ball of bast is placed in a pot of liquid vegetable dye prepared by Abe. "There can be no mistake in the color," he said. "Once the pulp is in to soak, the color cannot be corrected, although occasionally I give pulp two dye baths to create a special color. A good indigo is the hardest to achieve. The most important thing is to produce a good color and one that will not change with time. All my colors are absolutely fast and will fade only after extended exposure to bright sunlight. The papers I made years ago have not changed in hue, and I can still make the same colors today."

At a large, rectangular wooden vat, Abe carefully pushed up the sleeves of his blue and white cotton work jacket and reached for a huge, comblike wooden agitator to stir the plum-colored emulsion that filled the vat almost to the top. He fixed a wooden frame (*keta*) to two cords strung to a network of springy bamboo poles attached to the rafters. Opening the hinged frame, he stretched a bamboo screen (*su*) onto the vertical wooden bars of the lower half, snapped the open cover in place over the *su*, and lowered the entire mold into the vat. By shaking the frame, he allowed the pulp, starch, and water mixture in the vat to flow repeatedly over the screen as he moved the *keta* sideways and forward. His actions became gentler and, after half a dozen shakes, he lifted the frame from the liquid, tossed out the excess pulp, and let the water drain out through the screen; the supporting bamboo framework bent noticeably at first with the weight of the water. "By shaking the *su*, I let the fibers interlock," Abe explained.

"They get entangled and stick together to form a thin film, clinging to the *su* when the water runs out." He opened the frame and removed the *su*, which was now covered with a gelatinous-looking, watery sheet of pulp, then with a swift movement he flipped the fine bamboo screen upside down and peeled it off carefully, leaving a new sheet of glistening paper on top of a freshly made pile. "The *tororo* starch keeps the fibers in suspension. They don't stick together even after the water drains off," Abe remarked as he continued working over the vat, moving rhythmically and quickly, turning out a sheet of paper about every forty seconds. "The Japanese method makes it unnecessary to place cloth between each sheet of paper. The glutinous starch that oozes out of a pounded *tororo* root left in water is the Japanese secret. We use only a string along one deckle to keep the sheets separate for easier peeling off for drying," Abe raised his voice above the sound of water moving in his trough and the banging of the mold against the sides of the vat. "I turn out about three hundred sheets when I work the whole day, but some pulp mixtures are more difficult, and, of course, thin sheets of paper are harder to make than thick ones," he continued. "The proportion of pulp to *tororo* and water? That's almost impossible to answer and very difficult to teach, as my assistants will tell you. Books say about three parts pulp to seven parts water per vat, and then about three ladles of *tororo*, but it all depends on the type of paper. You have to learn to mix the emulsion by feel. Your hand will tell you if there is enough *tororo* to keep the fibers afloat. *Kozo* needs more than *mitsumata*, and finer *gampi* fibers are difficult to gauge. It's also important to mix the emulsion well and to judge when more pulp and starch must be added to the water. You can only learn by experience and also feeling the fibers float by."

At the next trough, a young apprentice smiled and agreed. "This young chap has learned quite quickly," Abe said. "This feels just about right, but maybe about half a ladle more of *tororo*?" A second apprentice gave another turn to the vise of a large, primitive screw press, and water dripped from a small pile of papers placed between several planks. Removing the excess water takes care and experience, since about seventy percent of the water must be removed from the wet paper, which has been allowed to drain naturally overnight. The technique is to press the moisture out gradually – a half-turn, then twenty minutes later a bit more pressure. Too much pressure will damage the paper.

Once pressed, individual sheets of damp paper are peeled off and spread on drying boards. A long soft brush of goat hair is usually used to iron the paper smoothly onto the drying boards, although some papers require careful massage with a round pad of lacquered paper-string wrapped in bamboo sheath, the unique *baren* that artists use in pressing paper to woodblocks.

Although Abe prefers the natural, sun drying method, he must also resort to indoor steam drying. In a light and humid room beyond the paper-making vats, a sweet-faced woman in her fifties spends her days brushing wet sheets of paper onto a vertical stainless steel griddle, which is steam-heated by a wood and coal fire. The sheets dry in minutes, and the woman's skill lies in the way in which she gently brushes the fragile, wet sheet of paper onto the griddle and the speed with which she does so. Three sheets on one side of the steam dryer, three on another and then it was time to peel off the first sheet. She pulled the crackly paper off the hot, steel plate delicately but firmly, working at a steady pace. She laughingly admitted that the work was sometimes uncomfortable in the heat of the summer, but very pleasant in the winter.

In addition to the *kozo*, *mitsumata*, and *gampi* fibers, Abe uses the tough *kuwa* (silk mulberry) bark for a few papers. In other papers, he adds a scattering of grasses, herbs, outer barks, and even kelp. A soft blue paper incorporating fine strips of green seaweed is a favorite of Abe's. In all his combinations, he maintains a natural feeling that reflects his sensitivity and conscientious respect for the materials. It is Abe's unique ability to reflect the beauty of nature in his craft that prompted his friend Bernard Leach to speak of the "friendly" character of Abe's papers and the honesty of the materials he uses. The natural colors and warm textures of Eishiro Abe's papers are an important contribution of Japan's long history as a country that produces, uses, and appreciates paper as an art form. A grandson who works beside him over the Abe vats is the paper artist's promise that Izumo paper will continue to be made.

Ayano Chiba   *Weaver and Dyer*   plates 10–17

"*Mukashi no mama, mukashi no mama*" ("Just as in the old days, just as in the old days"). Ayano Chiba slapped her kimonoed knees for emphasis as she nodded and smiled. The bright-eyed old lady sat in her small matted room with her legs tucked neatly under her diminutive frame.

"The Nara period? Well, I don't know much about all that although I suppose there must be some books in Kyoto that tell about all this weaving and dyeing," she said in the strong dialect of northern Honshu. "All I know is that I've been doing it for a long time and my family had done it for a long time and lots of people around here have done it for a long time. But I'm the only one left now. Guess there's no one foolish enough to take up this troublesome work these days. And it is lots of trouble you know, lots of trouble. But I've done it all my life, more or less, so I might as well keep at it. Reckon I couldn't just take it up at this age if I hadn't already been at it for years and years!"

Mrs. Chiba's career in dyeing covers fifty years. She did not start working with indigo on her own until she was thirty-four, having watched her parents and grandparents prepare and use the dye when she was a child. Her days at the spinning wheel and the loom started when she was a girl of fourteen. "Why, of course I started spinning when I was young, and I worked at the loom too. We were a farming family, but there was always a bit of time to spin and weave. I used to weave *asa* (hemp), cotton, and even silk. I wove many a bolt of silk material when I was a young girl, I'll tell you, many a bolt. I still weave silk now and then. Not cotton, though, and wool only once in a great while. I stick to *asa*."

The hemp that Mrs. Chiba grows today in the Kurikoma valley northwest of Sendai is hardly different from the hemp that provided fibers for the earliest textiles made by the people inhabiting the Japanese islands over two thousand years ago. The agrarian peoples of the Yayoi period are known to have used hemp and probably mulberry bark for plaited and later woven cloth. With the importation of many Korean and Chinese artisans and techniques in the fourth and fifth centuries, spinning, weaving, and dyeing developed rapidly. By the Nara period, textile craftsmen in the capital had been organized into guilds under imperial and governmental patronage. Artisans were also sent out into the provinces in 711 to teach weaving and dyeing throughout Japan. Eighth century fabrics that remain indicate that indigo was in use, the *Polygonium tinctorium* plant having been imported from China. As fine silk and cotton weaves proliferated, durable hemp materials were used by all classes.

"That *asa* growing so prettily in my plot up on the hill in June grew to be six *shaku* high (1.7 meters), lots taller than I am," Mrs. Chiba explained as she jumped up spryly to indicate its exact height, one long-fingered hand held high above her head. "We gathered the *asa* a few weeks ago, and I have just come from stripping off the skin down there in the paddy-field water. I'll clean the bumps off the bark on that plane there and then rinse off the strips and hang them up to dry." Bamboo poles draped with the long, buff-colored fibers hung beneath the veranda eaves of the main house. Next door is the small workshop-cottage in which Mrs. Chiba spends most of her time.

"This *asa* is very tough stuff. To soften it up before I spin it, I cook it in salt water and then in the water we pour off rice when we wash it. This bleaches it too, but I have to beat it by slapping it against the floor to get it soft enough to spin. Spinning takes a long time – my daughter and I do most of the spinning in the winter on those old spinning wheels just like the ones they used in the old days. It takes five basketfuls of thread to weave one bolt of kimono cloth and that's a lot of thread to weave, I'll tell you that. My daughter and I can spin enough for about four or five *tan* (bolts), and that is all we have time for. Once we spin it, we reel it around those baskets, those ones shaped like eel traps. We can soak the thread in water right on the baskets. I need wet thread for the weft. The warp has to be dry, you know, but the bobbins for the weft I keep wet and that makes a stronger cloth. This *asa* is very strong. Why, it'll last for three hundred years or so, or at least more than a hundred."

Mrs. Chiba's joyous account of preparing the hemp thread was punctuated frequently by her rolling laugh, the seldom encountered laugh of a truly happy person. Her enthusiasm for what she does is so clear in her vivacity and high spirits that anyone who has met her smiles at the very mention of her name. Her face is a network of cheerful wrinkles, her eyes are bright. Although she is slightly bent now and stands well under five feet, her mind is young and sharp.

"I used to be very tall," she said with a hearty chuckle, "That's why my hands are still so big I guess, but I've shrunk. I keep healthy by working. I eat everything – everything is delicious here – good rice, good vegetables. The only things I don't touch are saké and tobacco. I wake up about four in the morning and just wait for it be five so I can get up and get to work. I usually go to bed early, but do you know that sometimes I even switch on the electric light over my loom and weave as late as eleven at night? I like sumo and watch it once in a while, but most of that stuff on television is pretty bad, especially some of the naked dancing. Even if I can't understand what it's all about, I always listen to the news on the radio. I'm like a frog in a well – I'm just too busy where I am to hop out and go anywhere else. Oh, I've been to Sendai and once to Matsushima, but you know, I just can't get away. There's always so much to do here. My daughter has learned how to do most of this, but I still have to be right here to make sure it's all done correctly. Oh, it's a mighty difficult way to dye cloth, I'll tell you, mighty difficult," she said with that wonderful laugh lighting up her face.

"We're getting the seeds ready now for planting next year's crop of *ai* (indigo) in June, and all those bags up on shelves over the dye tubs are full of dried *ai* leaves. We pick the *ai* in late July, the second crop in September. It has nice pink blossoms, you know. We strip off the leaves and then I crumple them up and put them on rice-straw matting out in the sun to dry. In good weather, three days is enough. Then we store it in those net bags. I filled sixteen bags this year.

"But the bad summer weather ruined four bags. Mother was so unhappy I just couldn't look her in the face," her daughter, a bespectacled woman in her fifties, interjected. "She was miserable to have lost some of that *ai* – I just couldn't look her in the face – it was really dreadful."

Ignoring her daughter's mournful interruption, the old lady continued. "I'll explain our work as many times as you like, but you'll just never understand it until you do it. People can read about it, watch it, but they still don't get it. I say, better than trying to learn it, do it. Well, as I was saying, once the leaves are dry, we store them until January. We make the dye when it's very cold, and oh, it really does get cold here in January. But it's nice here in the winter, nice and quiet. Right after New Year's, I make a sort of bed out of lots of rice straw right down on the floor in front of the dyeing tub. Then I stuff some big bags made out of rice-straw matting with the *ai* leaves that have been washed in water but left wet. You have to stuff the bags full but not too much. Too little is no good either, just the right amount. We wrap the bags in more rice straw, put weights on top, and let the bags sit here on the dirt-floored section of the workroom. In a week, the leaves start to ferment, but I leave the bags without peeking in them for twenty days. Then I open up the bags and stir those fermenting leaves around very well – you have to be sure to give them a really good stir. Then, wrap them up again and put the stones or weights back on. The leaves have to sit like that for one hundred days altogether. The next job is to pound the leaves just the way you pound rice to make rice cakes at New Year's. We pound them with a wooden mallet in a stone mortar, in several batches, until it gets all into a ball. I break up these cakes of indigo paste into bits, about the size of a plum, and set the lumps out to dry for three to seven days, depending on the weather. And there you are – those are the *ai-dama* ["indigo balls"] that make the dye, just the way they did it in the old days!"

In addition to preparing the balls of indigo, Mrs. Chiba devotes some of the winter months to spinning and starts the weaving on her simple loom. Settling herself on the narrow plank seat of her low loom, she wove several inches, smiling the entire time. The huge shuttle, shiny from use, flew back and forth across the width of hemp; the two foot-rods controlling the harnesses clacked up and down; Mrs. Chiba's pull on the beater and its percussive bang punctuated her vigorous movements.

"How many threads in the warp? I don't know. I do it by feel – I just string out enough to make the cloth wide enough. Laying the warp is quite a job, but once that's done, the weaving is easy. It's just that I never seem to have time to spend a whole day at the loom. So much to do. Leaves to pick and then to turn; fibers to strip; guests to greet. You'd be surprised how many people come here to learn how to do this, but they'll just never know how unless they do it. I watched my parents do it, but I never knew how to do it until I just did it."

Mrs. Chiba explained that the stacks of charcoal by the house were oak wood. The charcoal would be burned in the *irori* (open hearth) and *hibachi* (brazier) in the main house all winter, as the ashes would supply the lye for the dye. "Not those white ashes, but those black bits at the bottom. We tried buying lye but it was no good, so we make it ourselves."

"I pray to the god of *ai* when I pick the indigo, and lots of other times too, especially when I'm making the dye," Mrs. Chiba said. "That wooden tub really is a bathtub but it's clean, had never been used when I got it.

I measure out the *ai-dama* and lye by weight, five parts to four. Then I pour in warm water – not too hot, not too cold, just right – just enough to cover the *ai* and lye. Then every day for a week I pour in a little more water – it can be hotter – until I get just the right amount. Too much is no good. Then I stir it very carefully and cover it. It has to sit for thirty days."

In order to dye a roll of the buff-colored hemp material, Mrs. Chiba inserts twelve flexible bamboo ribs along the selvage of the bolt, dips it into water, and then dips it into the vat of dye. "I put it in once for just the right amount of time – a few minutes – then take it out and let it drip back into the tub. Then in again, and once more. Once the dripping stops, I hang it up to dry. Once it dries, I give it three more dips. I do this dipping and drying six times, sometimes nine times, for each bolt of material. You see, I told you it was a difficult way of dyeing, didn't I? Just like in the old days!" she said laughing merrily. "*Ai* is really very strange stuff. Dyeing the cloth in *ai* toughens it and the *ai* also keeps it bug proof. *Ai* is very tricky to work with, you know. When I lift the cloth out of the vat, it's sort of green, but in the breeze it turns blue – right in front of my eyes it changes color. Then when the cloth has had the six or nine dyeings, I put it away. And do you know that that color deepens? It's remarkable. It gets to be a wonderful black-blue. If you put it away for six years or even three, the color will be just wonderful. It's amazing!"

Mrs. Chiba uses two wooden vats, the one made originally as a bathtub, which she bought when an old vat suddenly disintegrated, and the round wooden cask the village gave her to commemorate her designation as a Living National Treasure in 1955. She also uses an earthenware pot for dyeing small things such as skeins of wool or small pieces of cotton broad-cloth that she is often asked to dye for special orders. Once the dye is mixed in each of the containers, neither indigo nor lye nor water is added. "That's why that tub of dye is such a precious, precious thing, you see," she said emphatically. "If dust or hairs get in it, the dye is no good. But do you know that once in a while when groups come to see me we've found people putting their hands in my dye and mixing it? Isn't that terrible? Looking at the dye should be enough. Why, even I never put my hands in that dye. It's very precious. I pray to the indigo god and I'll tell you this, I keep the covers on those tubs now when I have visitors. The bubbles on it are a nice dark green. But I keep the dye covered. Imagine putting your hand into it."

From closets and drawers and cupboards and heaps, Mrs. Chiba and her daughter brought out various photographs and books and also two large stacks of stencils. "These stencils I've just always had. I got them from a dyer and they're all very old. I just use the ones I like. We make a paste resist using the flour from the wheat that was stacked up behind the *asa* plants in the field. Then my daughter and I stencil undyed cotton or hemp with the paste, dry the cloth, and then dye it in the *ai*. When I take the cloth down to the river in front to wash out the paste, the fish come by and nibble it off. I don't wash the cloth, the fish do. It's nice in the river in the summer – not too cold, very pleasant. I wash all the indigo material there too. And I'll tell you that when I've washed it and dried it, no *ai* is going to come off on anyone's underwear or skin. My dye is absolutely fast, no rubbing off ever. Just as in the old days."

16

Kei Fujiwara *Potter – Bizen* plates 18–21

"This clay is the best clay in the world." Kei Fujiwara emphatically slapped the glistening mound of dark gray clay that sat on his potter's wheel. "There is not better clay anywhere. We dig it up from beneath the rice paddies of Imbe. Just feel it. Yes, it can be described as creamy and silky to the touch, but what is important to the potter is that it has great plasticity."

Fujiwara glanced out of the window of his spartan workshop attached to his luxurious new home in the outskirts of the village of Bizen in the Imbe area of Okayama Prefecture. His eyes half-closed beneath his bushy, sloping eyebrows, he absently rubbed his hands together in the wooden basin of water beside him. He gazed intently at the green hills and deep blue waters of the Inland Sea below his garden. Turning back to his wheel, he embraced the pile of clay with wet hands. The electric motor hummed softly. Expression left his face. His fingers made sticky noises as they squeezed the mass of clay. He drew the whirling clay up with his hands, and then his thumbs formed a well in the gray mound, his strong fingers guiding it up into an ever-changing cylinder. Without removing his hands from the splattering gray mass, the potter stood up. Leaning over his work, the small, spare man seemed to pour the strength of his entire body into the vase he was fashioning. He sat down again, cleaned his hands, and then dove into the clay once more – once again he rose, once again he sat. After five minutes of work he gave a low, growling laugh. "There," he said, "the vase is done. I work so fast that I almost feel sorry for the people who purchase my pieces, considering how much I enjoy working at the wheel and how little time it actually takes to shape the piece. If I worked all day, I'd fill the whole room. I am very fortunate, I think, to be able to work with a material I love and know well and to make things I like to make. There is something special about this clay. Being a potter is a splendid occupation."

The dense, unglazed stoneware that Fujiwara produces is the same type of Bizen ware that has been made in the area for almost one thousand years. Fujiwara is proud of Bizen ware's long and uninterrupted history. This pottery resisted foreign influences throughout its development, remaining faithful to the techniques and shapes that have made it distinctive. Most pieces might generally be described as brown by the novice, but on longer acquaintance, one can distinguish a whole spectrum

17

of tones of brown, partaking fully of muted grays, reds, yellows, and greens. Bizen pots often have rivulets, smears, and patches of matte black, mustard, plum, and light blue hues. Although some pieces are very smooth, most Bizen ware has a pleasantly rough texture (*zangurishita*) that has great appeal in Japan. The feel of a water container or a teabowl is an important feature of its beauty, according to the Japanese sense of aesthetics, and the *zangurishita* quality of Bizen pieces has excited generations of tea devotees, who found the natural roughness compatible with the spirit that has pervaded the world of tea for some four hundred years. This rustic quality is enhanced by the fact that the only glaze that Bizen pieces wear is a natural or accidental glaze acquired in the kiln during the long firing process. This glaze results from the reaction of the clay, which is relatively low in iron content (about three percent as compared to six percent in Mashiko clay) but high in organic impurities, to the temperature, smoke, and wood ash in the kiln atmosphere.

"Since Bizen ware is naked pottery, the character of the clay and the potter show clearly," Fujiwara remarked, cradling a large cup of green tea in his sturdy hands. "The glazes used on other types of ceramics might be compared to the white powder that a country lass uses to cover her natural, sunburnt beauty. In Bizen ware, there is virginal beauty and innocent freshness. The beauty of true Bizen ware lies in its boldness and simplicity. It is direct and natural. It is strong, plain, and honest. It does not pretend."

Leaving the cool workshop, Fujiwara relaxed in his Western style sitting room, sipping frothy green tea served by his wife in large Fujiwara bowls. Fujiwara wore his heavy, dark, silk kimono casually. He sprawled loosely in his chair, then tucked one leg beneath him, finally bringing the other knee up to shoulder level and leaning lazily against it. His speech is low and slurred, and has an unmistakable *zangurishita* quality to it. Whether with family or guests, he talks in an offhand manner, as his heavy-lidded gaze wanders from the huge seven-hundred-year-old Tamba water container outside the sliding door to the Miro painting on the wall, then to the piece of Inca weaving covering the low table in front of him. But behind his sleepy, careless manner lies the active mind of an intellectual, and with a sudden searing gaze Fujiwara launches into a discussion of Shakespeare, Whitman, or Chekhov, the spirit of tea or Christianity, the beauty of Korean pottery or Marilyn Monroe, the delight of a particular violin concerto or his favorite brand of saké. Mercurial but unpretentious, he lets a conversation drift then suddenly veer. A pronouncement on Zen, a humorous account of a drinking episode, an analysis of tradition, and remarks on his enjoyment of the company of lively ladies follow one another in fast sequence. His curiosity is as honest as is his disdain for the artificial.

"These young Japanese who go abroad to study pottery! It's backwards. They would do better to study pottery here in Japan. They must become familiar with their own country's artistic tradition. But it is not enough for them to imitate the traditional. Tradition is the foundation on which a potter must build his work, but he must not merely copy old pieces."

Fujiwara feels that most of the forty artist-potters who make Bizen

stoneware today are merely imitating the pieces produced during the Momoyama period, when Bizen became popular among cultivated people because of the interest shown in it by tea masters and by the great general Hideyoshi Toyotomi, who was also a tea enthusiast. At the famous Kitano tea party the general gave for thousands in 1587, this fascinating historical figure used several pieces of Bizen pottery. Moreover, his remains are said to have been buried in a Bizen container. The vogue for Bizen ware increased during the first half of the Edo period, and the Bizen potters who had made simple bowls, tea storage jars, and grinding bowls accepted orders for the water containers, flower vases, tea caddies, and teabowls required for the increasingly popular tea ceremony.

Fujiwara is especially interested in the pottery of the earlier Kamakura period, about the end of the twelfth century. Bizen is known as one of the "Six Ancient Kilns," centers of ceramic production still active (with the exception of Echizen) that seem also to have been major ceramic centers of medieval Japan. These six provincial kilns developed strong local characteristics, although all six had based their pottery traditions on the dense gray Sue ware, which replaced the low-fired Yayoi pottery in about the fourth century. Techniques of firing the hard, gray Sue pots in an *anagama* (literally, "hole kiln") and the shapes of early Sue pieces were the result of cultural exchanges with Korea in the pre-Nara periods, but the potters of Japan adapted and assimilated the mainland influences to produce a ware that was soon characteristically Japanese. By the ninth century, some fourteen hundred kilns were producing a great variety of Sue pottery throughout Japan. Ceramic production dwindled in the late Heian period, and the Six Ancient Kilns seem to have become the main active pottery producing areas in the Kamakura period. (Recent archaeological finds indicate that ceramic activity was undoubtedly more widespread.) By that time Bizen ware had developed a refinement and quality that set it apart from the wares of the other five old kilns – Seto, Tokoname, Tamba, Echizen, and Shigaraki. There is no doubt that the unusual clay of the area, the tight guild of hereditary potters, the interest and protection of the great Hideyoshi, and the patronage of the feudal house of Ikeda all contributed to the unique development of Bizen pottery.

Although Fujiwara was born in the area of Bizen, he is not descended from generations of potters as are most of today's creators of Bizen ware. The second son of a farmer, young Fujiwara spent his school days writing poetry and enjoying pranks and sports, not interested in the kilns that surrounded him. Fujiwara believes that a man need not be brought up in a family of potters to do good work and, further, that a potter is much more likely to be a good one if he does not live entirely in a world of wheel, fire, and clay.

"What is important in being a potter is not formal schooling, but general experience and education. A person of cultural refinement and various intellectual pursuits is a truly educated man, whatever his actual schooling. In addition to culture, a strong personality is a requirement for a potter. Technique is not important. Any worker can acquire techniques. Techniques and great numbers of tools are for the lowly worker in crafts, not for the real potter. It is refinement and character that distinguish the true potter from the man who merely works at making pots. He must be someone who experiences and recognizes what is good, whether in music, painting, literature, or philosophy. By absorbing these into his being, he can put strength and character into what he makes out of clay."

Fujiwara's formal education came to an abrupt halt when he was sixteen, after the officials at the high school he attended discovered that a recent absence had involved saké and feminine company. Instead of being suspended, as his furious father had envisaged, the school dismissed the young man but gave him a graduation diploma. His first job was teaching, but he continued to write. His poetry and essays caught the attention of writers and intellectuals, and Fujiwara came to meet authors, poets, critics, and philosophers throughout Japan. Moving to Tokyo, he did museum work, tried his hand at editing a series of small, unsuccessful literary publications, dabbled in Christianity, socialism, oil painting, and the violin. He wrote serial stories, movie scenarios, essays, poems, and newspaper articles, read widely in world literature, and finally even peddled underwear in a street stall to support his pleasure-loving ways. Exhausted at last at the pace of a life of insecurity and apparent failure, he returned to Bizen, where a friend urged him to work with clay instead of words. Fujiwara now feels that he was saved as a human being by exchanging his writer's brush for the potter's wheel.

"I was forty when I first felt clay, and the minute I touched it, I felt something special. I knew nothing about turning a wheel, choosing clay, using a kiln, but thanks to good friends who taught and helped me, I soon picked up the techniques and became absolutely dedicated." Those were difficult years, since Fujiwara and his wife were poor and had two children to support. The boys often went with their father into the hills to look for firewood for the kiln.

"Bizen is an ideal place for a potter, because there is plenty of superb clay and abundant pine wood for fuel. In addition to that, the climate is good – it is mild, we get little rain, and the winds are seldom strong. Humidity, temperature, and air currents have a great influence on how the kiln operates. For a successful firing, good weather is a must. I used to listen to weather reports, but I don't trust them anymore. I fire only once a year, in mid November, when the weather is ideal. Come back in November for the kiln opening," he said gruffly. "It's interesting. Come."

Fujiwara's daughter-in-law appeared with more tea and with plates of deep, purple Okayama grapes splashed with water. The bright green of the tea set off the orange of bowls. Wetting the fruit plates added another dimension to their brown color.

"Of course I never know exactly how the fire will treat my pieces of clay," Fujiwara continued. "About half of the pieces I fire I consider failures, and only about ten percent can be considered good. My son, Yu, fires twice a year, but he is young and can work harder. I am seventy-three, so I spend a lot of time relaxing, drinking, and enjoying myself these days."

Yu Fujiwara, Fujiwara's eldest son and a prize-winning Bizen potter, lives with his pretty wife and two children in a large house in his parents' compound. After working for many years at his father's side, he now throws his pots in his own workshop. A younger son, also a potter, lives away from home and works in a tradition that uses some applied glazes.

"Our clay is processed completely by hand," explained Yu, an intense, stocky man in his late thirties. "Dug from below Imbe rice fields in the winter, the clay is weathered by several years exposure to rain, wind, snow, and sun. The dried clay-rich dirt is pulverized by hand by apprentices and examined particle by particle. White and gray portions, stones, sand, and all foreign matter are picked out, leaving only the good black clay, which is sieved, mixed with water, settled in covered tanks, drained, foot-kneaded, and finally mixed with a small amount of mountain clay. The clay is then packed into shallow, wide earthenware dishes to stiffen and season out-of-doors on roofed shelves and then repacked into large cubes and left to ripen in a special storehouse for two or three years before the potter kneads the amount required and throws it on his wheel. Bizen clay has great viscosity and intense elasticity. It is responsive to the potter's fingers, but retains the form he gives it. It is absolutely superb clay," Yu remarked. "The best," muttered his father, "the best."

"The way we load the kiln is very, very important," the elder Fujiwara continued. "Since the color and texture of the finished pot depend entirely on its position in the kiln and its proximity to the heat, I have to work out the loading plan very carefully. It makes my head ache to think about it," Fujiwara said with a dry laugh. "The order and pattern of packing the pots, vases, bowls, and cups into the kiln, the height of the slabs on which they sit – all these factors must be considered. Fire always follows the easiest route, and the path of the heat through the kiln shows in the natural glazes that result. Large, round *tsubo* (jars) are often placed next to thinner *tokkuri* (saké bottles) or small tea cups. Saké cups are sometimes placed over the mouth of a vase, next to a jar, or directly on a platter, and a round shadow or pattern on the surface of the covered piece is the result. Rice-straw rope is bound on some pieces in order to produce red streaks or lines where the ash fuses with the clay. Pine wood ash from the wood fuel used to fire the kiln and rice-straw ash are carried by the kiln drafts, settling on the shoulders of large round vases or in the teabowls to achieve a natural speckled or sesame seed (*goma*) pattern.

Loading the kiln may take a week or more. Fujiwara uses gas to warm the kiln for the first two or three days, and then pine wood is inserted in varying amounts, but always by hand, for the next nine days. Close to three truckloads of red pine wood are required for each firing, because a temperature of approximately 1320°C must be reached gradually and then maintained. The kiln is left to cool for six or seven days.

"People say my saké bottles are my best pieces because I like saké so much," Fujiwara said. "A Bizen *tokkuri* mellows with use and improves the flavor of the saké." In addition to saké bottles and cups, Fujiwara makes a variety of large pots, whose forms are based on early grain jars and tea storage jars. His rectangular saké bottles, slab platters, square vases, round water containers for the tea ceremony, cylindrical vases with and without handles, teabowls in a variety of shapes and sizes all display a distinctive honesty with variations in color and texture that are as subtle and unexpected as the changes in mood of the potter himself.

The country people of Mashiko were suspicious of the educated, well-traveled Tokyo potter who chose their pottery village for the site of his kiln in 1924. Today, Shoji Hamada, who is known all over the world as a folk potter, speaks affectionately of "my Mashiko," and the 19,000 inhabitants of the town have come at last to regard him with fond pride as one of their own.

The anonymous potters of Mashiko, 120 kilometers northeast of Tokyo, have more than a century's tradition of producing simple, sturdy pieces of glazed stoneware for kitchen and table, using the local iron-rich clay. Despite the taste and high standards evident in Mashiko folk pottery, this ware had not at the time of Hamada's arrival been accorded the interest given the wares of older traditional provincial kilns such as Shigaraki, Seto, and Bizen, so favored by tea devotees. The shapes, designs and glazes of Mashiko rice bowls and teapots are the products of what Hamada calls the "unconscious creativity" of the craftsman. Potters never thought of producing artistic signed pieces; the village artisans simply produced crockery to be used. It was these townspeople who were convinced that the young Hamada's cosmopolitan education acquired in a Tokyo technical college, a Kyoto ceramic research institute, and kilns in Okinawa and England would make him critical of the Mashiko folk pottery tradition. Instead, his neighbors were won over slowly by his robust honesty and natural warmth. His gradual recognition by Japanese and foreign collectors did not alter his appreciation of the unpretentious products of Mashiko kilns and the craftsmen who made them.

"When I first came here, many local people refused to be seen speaking to me," Hamada related as he strode along in his large compound of old farm buildings and kilns. Dressed in one of the informal but handsome homespun outfits in which he customarily works and receives guests, he walked with a firm step and a wide buoyant stride. His round face broke frequently into large smiles; he paused to scold a barking dog with a word and a laugh and to admire the ripe black figs being gathered by a gardener precariously perched on a tall bamboo ladder. He stopped to greet an elderly visiting couple, and his robustness seemed to accentuate their frailty. He turned to walk down a stone-paved path, his large wooden clogs clattering authoritatively. "The young sons of Mashiko potters dared to visit me only after dark," Hamada continued. "Gifts of chocolate or tomatoes, which I was eager to share with people in Mashiko, were greeted with great suspicion and usually refused." He laughed quietly as he recalled his early years in Mashiko almost fifty years before. "It took a long time to win the confidence of these good people. The fact that I used the clay from the local cooperative, worked with the same glazes, and fired in the same type of kiln gradually helped convince them of my sincerity and honesty. Only after six years did the village decide I should be allowed to buy some land. I built a house and a small *nobori-gama* (multichambered climbing kiln) and for a modest sum I was able to purchase this wonderful old country *nagaya-mon* (large gateway with living quarters) and have it moved here from a nearby village." The solid *nagaya-mon* is constructed of plaster, wood, and thatch and seems to have been born where it now stands along the dirt road leading past Hamada's property. Rooms flanking the large gate now serve as pottery storerooms.

Walking through the gate Hamada stood in the light rain a minute or two to enjoy the view of mist-shrouded mountains beyond an expanse of carefully tended vegetable patches and rice paddies. "Even in the rain this is a lovely view," he said. Hamada did not merely look at the view: he partook of it and was refreshed. "Look at the farmer over there picking vegetables and you will see how I am now when I open a kiln after a firing. I am like that farmer pulling potatoes out of the ground. When I first started potting, I used to get excited over firings, but I have learned that what I must do is simply use the best materials, put my spirit into producing an honest piece, and then just wait to see what happens in the kiln. The clay, the glazes, the wood, the condition of the kiln, the temperature, wind, humidity – all of these play a role in producing a piece of pottery. Of course I make mistakes, but we learn from mistakes; I destroy about a third of the five thousand pots I make every year, and only about five hundred reach exhibitions. Another third of my annual output goes to folkcraft shops and the art sections of a few department stores. I don't make any fuss over the pots I destroy, although I notice that some potters break them in front of press cameras. I disagree with that. I break my pots at midnight, so to speak. My failures are important to me. I used to throw

them all away, but now more than ever before I find I want to study them. Often, nowadays, I do get to succeed," he mused aloud as if he were talking about someone else. He turned to lead the way up the hill to the main workshop.

In the long gray workshed whose bamboo ceiling rests on huge hand-hewn beams, Hamada works at one of the seven potters' wheels recessed slightly below the wooden work platform. One of Hamada's sons was throwing tea cups on a foot wheel next to his father's work area. Several assistants worked at molding and kneading.

"I only work about ten days a month nowadays, since I seem to be busy on committees and various projects. I rise very early and can throw for two or three hours before breakfast. I often return to my wheel after supper to work until almost midnight. Today I will put overglaze designs on some pieces that I threw some time ago and just recently glazed."

Hamada settled himself cross-legged on a worn cushion placed next to his wheel. Picking up a tea ceremony bowl that had already received an off-white glaze coat, he examined it carefully, holding it in his short, strong fingers with delicacy and confidence. Talking softly to himself, he worked out the combination of enamel overglazes he planned to apply, stroking an imaginary design or two on the bowl with his finger. He plunged the long, bamboo-handled brush into a porcelain mortar containing the glaze and firmly painted several lines on the cup. His control of the limp tip of the brush, heavy with thick glaze, was sensitive and sure. He next used a shorter, firmer brush filled with reddish glaze and painted alternate sections of the bowl with thick, square daubs of glaze. He worked swiftly but never hurriedly, the supple brush held lightly between his thumb and middle finger. In half an hour, he decorated seven or eight tea ceremony bowls, three incense boxes, several water droppers, and a small plate. In a later decorating session he spent an hour or so applying red and green overglaze designs to three dozen *kaki* vases, saké pourers, and saké cups. The *kaki* (literally, "persimmon") glaze is a lustrous reddish brown characteristic of Mashiko ware and perfected by Hamada. Combining the pulverized, iron-bearing red clay of Mashiko with ashes, Hamada creates a glaze that fires to a satiny chestnut brown. Many of his *kaki* pieces first receive a white glaze coat and over that a wax resist pattern of circles or rectangles; when the *kaki* is applied, it does not adhere to the wax, which melts in firing, leaving circles or rectangles of white. It is in these white areas that Hamada applies the bright overglaze enamel designs, usually in red or green.

"Very colorful," Hamada remarked cheerfully as he daubed patches of various glaze on a shallow teabowl. "This will have designs in yellow, red, green, and purple. Sometimes visitors say I paint quickly," Hamada continued in carefully enunciated English, "but I say, I am not quick. For each stroke, sixty years plus one second."

An assistant, with whom Hamada chatted off and on, hovered nearby and took decorated pieces from the dimly lit, dirt-floored workshop to the small overglaze kiln in the next building. The pieces would be fired for six hours at a relatively low temperature of about 800° C, just enough to fuse the overglaze enamel without ruining the other glazes. Glazes are fired at about 1300° C for forty-eight hours of carefully controlled firing. The workshop floor was crowded with drying boards on which stood rows of large plates, big round vases, smaller square vases, and bowls of various sizes, all of which would be receiving glazes in the next few days.

Hamada uses iron, cobalt, and copper glazes as well as rice-straw ash and wood ash glazes. Brushing, trailing, and dipping in various combinations are all used to apply glaze. On some large pieces, Hamada drips the glaze from a metal dipper to create an overall design. This strong, abstract, trailed glaze pattern is a characteristic Hamada design. His crisscrossing lines, freely dripped stripes and loops are often imitated, but not with the power that Hamada achieves with this seemingly casual technique. "I do not think much about glazes or color when I am throwing a piece," Hamada said. "A little, yes, but not too much. I can get new ideas by working out the colors in my mind later. If I think about designs when I'm throwing, there is the danger that I keep repeating what I've done before. When I am painting, I sometimes leave a funny space, without knowing just why. I just leave it, and after the piece is fired, I sometimes find it succeeds, although while decorating, the design developed unconsciously."

The tea ceremony has inspired much of Japan's artistic development, but many older tea devotees do not care for Hamada's tea ceremony bowls. They prefer the very old, traditional style bowls. "Young people, however, like to use my teabowls," Hamada remarked, "because they like a more natural tea ceremony. I think that the great tea master Sen-no-Rikyu had a very good eye, and I admire him very much, but he was too proud. When he tried to order potters to make bowls according to his wishes, he failed. His heart was not good. Gradually, tea masters emphasized irregularity to the point of unnatural deformity. Tea became too tasty." Hamada spoke with quiet emphasis and conviction, but his tone of voice was friendly. Hamada manipulates even the English language as firmly as he does his clay, with unmistakable meaning.

"Pottery is at its highest point since even the Edo period," he went on. "At least the highest point since the Meiji era. In the Edo period we had the five great potters – Koetsu, Ninsei, Kenzan, Eisen, and Mokubei. In our era, we have already produced two great potters – Kenkichi Tomimoto and Kanjiro Kawai. There are others, but they are mountains or hills under the clouds. Tomimoto and Kawai rise above the clouds."

One of Japan's greatest potters and the creator of some of the most famous teabowls, Koetsu (1558–1637) worked in the style of the Raku family potters in Kyoto, but his strong forms and subtle glazes made his work a unique contribution to Japanese ceramic tradition. Ninsei worked in Kyoto in the middle and late seventeenth century; and his signed teabowls and round vases are notable for the colorful designs he applied to pottery in overglaze enamels, which until that time had generally been used only on porcelain. This highly decorative polychrome pottery inspired the versatile Kenzan to try his hands at this craft. Considered by most people the towering figure in the history of Japanese ceramics, Kenzan (1663–1743) combined a mastery of color glazing with a highly inventive sense of design and boldness tempered by delicacy. The Chinese porcelain

techniques of the Ming dynasty inspired Eisen (1753–1811) and his pupil Mokubei (1767–1833) to reproduce and adapt them for Japan.

Korean pottery rather than Chinese porcelain inspired both Hamada and his great friend and colleague in the folk art movement, Kanjiro Kawai (1890–1966), and its founder, Soetsu Yanagi (1889–1961): they shared a great admiration for early Yi dynasty pieces, which Hamada today includes among his favorite ceramics. Kawai's skilled brush, interesting forms, and the variety and quality of his glazes, especially his blues, copper-reds and browns, make his work memorable. Although Tomimoto was also greatly influenced by Yi pieces and was active in the early folkcraft movement with Hamada and Kawai, his style gradually changed and his refined work in enameled porcelains as well as his elegant brushwork earned him the designation of a Living National Treasure. Hamada rates Tomimoto as an outstanding potter, but neither he nor Kawai agreed with Tomimoto's decision to sign his pieces. Hamada continues to produce only unsigned pots.

Hamada's designation as the "holder of a traditional technique registered as an Intangible Cultural Property" is in contradiction to his craftsman's credo and his belief in an intuitive approach to beauty. He is firm in his preference for recognition of work rather than the bestowal of honors. "I prefer what Soetsu Yanagi used to call beauty without measure, without ranking."

By maintaining his basic simplicity and honesty, Hamada inspires many young potters to follow his example of purity of purpose. His fame has focused interest generally on the town of Mashiko and its wares and has also served to encourage the kiln workers there to continue to produce the pickle dishes, the beanpaste storage jars, and the tea cups and everyday ware that are still made anonymously and that continue to combine beauty with utility. Of the 130 some individual potters in Mashiko, many have come to take on the artist's custom of signing his work, but most remain loyal to the folk art tradition.

"Many people come to my Mashiko not by eye but by ear," Hamada said, "but it is very important that people choose pottery by eye, not by name or price. Judge a piece with your heart, not your brain. For young potters to develop, good critics are needed. We have not had a truly good critic since Soetsu Yanagi died. He had a pure eye. He saw with his heart. Critics today judge with their brains. Too much head, not enough heart. That is not good for the potters or the public. Young potters today often sell rather well very early in their careers; this can be dangerous if they continue to make pots just to sell them. They do not grow as potters. But there are many potters working today, and we must wait and see if they will be able to get through. A young potter must work, work, work. Less talk and more work. He must use his hands, his head, and his heart, but heart is the most important. As he develops, his strength will come through in his work, but it is important for him to dig deep down beneath his own feet to find spring water. This is better than finding a section of the river of tradition that has already become unclear and weak. True tradition never comes from water flowing above the ground: it comes from underneath the ground, from a man's own experience. Individualism is important, and without it we cannot do any good work in this age. To find real individualism does not mean we must follow the new fashions but rather the old way, the classic way. The classic way is much, much better. What is classic is always new; fashions are always old. A man must study beauty with his own eyes. Today there is too much dependence on knowledge, and knowledge is not good enough. We must know from the heart and from the neck down. The head is not necessary for this kind of knowing. When we study something, we must digest everything slowly and carefully and then produce results. Some potters take a safe path to sell, and so they fail or become too ambitious or too proud.

"I think potters must not study only pots. They should look at sculpture, at woodwork, clay figures, and tapestries. I get inspiration from furniture, textiles, drawings, and other things."

In the handsome old farmhouse where Hamada keeps his collection of artifacts from all over the world, he commented on the simple beauty of an early Shaker cupboard, a heavy wooden chest from Spain, and several Windsor chairs. "But this is the best," he said, picking up a weathered wooden milking stool found in the Pyrenees. "Wonderful – so strong, so direct – functional and beautiful." The tatami-matted rooms are piled with chests, boxes, plates, baskets, pots, paintings, and hangings. Among these treasures is one of Hamada's own twenty-six-inch platters with amber glaze trailed across a rich, black background. "Even this plate that I made twenty years ago has matured so that it does not look new at all," Hamada said. He turned to examine in turn an ancient Coptic textile, an Eskimo soapstone etching, an Inca drawing of "a funny, funny animal," an Australian Aborigine painting, several Mexican clay animals, pieces from Spain, Taiwan, Korea, Colombia, and English slipware plates. "This Norwegian food vessel of wood was my favorite piece," the potter said, "until I found this very old wooden bowl from Samarkand." Each of his artifacts fascinates Hamada, who thrives on other cultures, other ages, and other media. "My friend Shiko Munakata, the artist, calls this my endless collection, but I disagree. I tell him, since I have consumed the being of these treasures, there is nothing left." Outside the treasure house, Hamada glanced back. Framed on the veranda were a black Eames chair and an Okinawan funerary urn.

In his eight-chambered *nobori-gama* (climbing kiln) Hamada fires about one thousand pieces at a time twice a year. The small two-chambered kiln he uses for salt-glazing: the introduction of salt during firing produces an orange-peel-like surface texture that he likes. At the gatehouse storerooms, two rows of Hamada pots were set out along the path: paper in hand, Hamada walked slowly past the teabowls, plates, and vases, pausing, judging, winnowing the ranks. He rejected a tea cup because, he said, the glaze was a bit weak; a tea ceremony bowl was dismissed for being "sweet" and a vase for being "dull"; a plate lost out because its blue was too harsh. In just twenty minutes the potter had decided on the fifty pieces to comprise his next exhibition.

"And now it is time to get back to work. My annual December exhibit has seventy-seven teabowls in it. One for every year of my life."

Heiro Kitagawa   *Weaver*   plates 28–35

It was in Nishijin, the northwestern sector of Kyoto, that the House of
Tawaraya grew, and it is in Nishijin today that the seventeenth generation
of Tawaraya silk weavers, Heiro Kitagawa, works the looms with his son.
Five centuries ago, in 1467, at the start of the disastrous civil strife that
introduced over a hundred years of turmoil, this greatest of Japan's silk-
weaving establishments was founded in a sector of the city, known to the
participants of the Onin Wars as the Western Camp (Nishi Jinya). The
artistic development of that troubled century – the painting, ceramics,
architecture, landscape gardening, the Noh drama, tea ceremony, and
applied arts – was astonishing, and is the more to be wondered at accompanied as it was by civil discord and political confusion. While warlords
thrust and parried in city and province, and Kyoto temples, shops, and
homes burned to the ground not far from the palace inhabited by a virtually
powerless emperor, the effete shogun, Yoshimasa Ashikaga, retreated

first to his Muromachi palace and then to his mansion in the eastern hills (Higashiyama) of Kyoto to participate in tea ceremonies, Noh plays, and Zen discussions.

From the beginning, the Tawaraya silk establishment produced silks for the imperial family, the aristocracy, and the ruling houses of Japan. Ceremonial dress for palace rituals as well as robes for the clergy and hangings for Shinto shrines and Buddhist temples have always been woven by Tawaraya according to strict requirements. Exquisite Noh costumes continue to be a consuming interest of the masters of Tawaraya and a specialty of the great house: subtly luxurious Nishijin brocades have been a favorite with generations of tea ceremony devotees. "Although it is important to go on weaving fine silks for the court, the shrine, tea ceremony house, and the Noh stage, I also want to introduce the beauty of Japan's heritage of textile arts to the ordinary person," Kitagawa said. "I do not believe that this brocade or that design is good just because it is old but I think one should learn to recognize the good qualities of what is old and to select certain features of antique textiles for their artistic value rather than their historic value."

Dressed in a dark silk kimono of restrained elegance, Kitagawa sat at a low Japanese table in his small upstairs sitting room. A single large purple morning glory had been placed in a vase at the head of the steep stairs leading from the entrance hall below. In one corner of the room stood a two-panel screen decorated with squares of fabric of ancient design that Kitagawa had woven himself as a research project. The view from corner windows is of Mt. Hiei, whose sacred and historical connotations are now marred by ropeways, viewing platforms, and hotels. Adjoining the sitting room, a large room was decorated with framed awards and pictures, books and stacked rolls of materials; there, too, was the crib and the bright toys of Kitagawa's grandchild. Speaking with youthful enthusiasm and a crusader's fervor, Kitagawa was quick to illustrate his remarks with rolls of silk flung casually onto the tatami or with books chosen from the many-shelved cabinet behind him.

"It is important, although sometimes difficult, to link the traditional and the contemporary," Kitagawa said. "Sometimes I choose an eighth century texture or an antique pattern and reconstruct and reproduce it because it seems to fit the times, but in other cases, I will adapt an old weave or traditional design to be used and appreciated today."

Renowned now for his studies of ancient weaving techniques, and designated in 1956 and 1961 a "holder of a traditional technique registered as an Intangible Cultural Property" for his re-creation of certain historic weaves, Kitagawa's academic career was devoted to painting. "But once I started working at the looms with my father in the family business, I became fascinated with textures and weaves. I saw fabrics in museums and read about costumes in old documents or novels and was determined to find out how they were woven. My father was basically a craftsman, as was his father before him, all the way back to the founding of Tawaraya. But he did research in order to repair some of the old fabrics in the Shoso-in collection of imperial treasures, and I was able to study the fabrics there also. I learned from my father's training as a weaver and also from the many scholars who came to study those treasures of the Nara period. Thus I was led into the study of fabrics of many eras and many countries." From a folder filled with paper packets Kitagawa unfolded several to reveal wisps of patterned brocade and scraps of striped damask. "These are bits of cloth woven in the Asuka and Nara eras. My father collected some of these bits and pieces, and I have added many more, finding them here and there, in old temples for instance. I study them carefully and eventually I am able to determine the weave and to work out how the loom should be structured to produce a replica." The tattered scraps, more than twelve hundred years old, date back to the peak of traffic on the Silk Road across Central Asia, yet despite their age they showed clear tones of purple, plum, orange, yellow, and many shades of green. Chinese silk had been exported westward to the aristocratic ladies of the Roman Empire since early in the second century, and eastward to Japan by the third century. Chinese and Korean rulers used to send silkworms, skeins or bolts of silk, or even a weaver or two as gifts to Japanese emperors, but indigenous sericulture was encouraged in the third and fourth centuries, and soon weavers occupied a privileged position among artisans in Japan. Luxurious silks woven in China reached Japan in large quantities in the Asuka and Nara periods and inspired native development of textiles. With the personal encouragement of Emperor Kotoku, special looms were built in 645 to produce multicolored brocades. By 701, immigrant Korean and Chinese weavers had been assimilated; they were joined by Japanese craftsmen in a guild of weavers established with the blessing of the court, and Japan embarked on a golden age of textile artistry.

Nara courtiers were luxuriously robed in bright silks emulating the splendors of T'ang dynasty civilization, and palace ceremonies and religious rituals were conducted against a background of dazzling brocades and tapestries. Among the splendid examples in the Shoso-in are *nishiki*, the generic term for patterned silk woven with threads of many colors. In some, the warp threads and in others, the weft provided the designs of stripes, hunting scenes, and stylized flowers. *Aya*, a silk damask of one color, features woven geometric designs against a twilled ground, and the trio of fine silk gauzes, *ra*, *sha*, and *ro*, show variations of open weave. The remarkable tapestry weave (*tsuzure-ori*) is a standard Tawaraya technique today, and for this brocade, the weaver, rather than using a single weft thread that passes through the whole width of the warp, and surfaces only when needed, uses a number of shuttles for the weft, each one passing a certain thread back and forth over only the section necessary for the design, the threads intertwining where colors meet.

"My research, especially handling the old Shoso-in fabrics, enabled me to reconstruct the twelve-hundred-year-old secret of weaving *ra*," the scholar-weaver said. "Its stiff-textured open weave is achieved by an intricate schedule of intertwined warp threads of very fine silk and a tightly woven weft. Our looms weave traditional *ra* today, and I have also adapted the weave to a larger scale, using heavier threads, in order to produce *obi* (kimono sashes). Since a skilled craftsman can only weave seven centimeters a day, our production cannot keep up with the demand." Kitagawa unrolled a plum-colored *obi* of *ra* weave like a densely woven, geometrically patterned lace. "Women like these *obi* because they are stiff enough to support, but they have enough give to be comfortable: this barely noticeable elasticity is a characteristic of a properly woven silk *obi*."

Since woven silk was produced only for the aristocracy until some four hundred years ago, the weavers of Nara moved to Kyoto with the court when the emperor established the capital there in 794. The passionate and intricate aesthetic that characterized Heian society is well recorded by Lady Murasaki in *The Tale of Genji* and Sei Shonagon in her *Pillow Book*. The "rule of taste" and exaggerated emphasis on color produced great advances in weaving and dyeing. Kitagawa has several pieces of *aya* (silk twill) used for the many-layered outfits worn by Kyoto nobility; courtiers of both sexes chose the colors of their robes knowing that the way they combined and layered the colors and textures would be noticed by all. *Aya* of various textures and weaves identical to those worn in the Heian court are being woven for palace rituals to this day. A sample of material recently woven for an imperial wedding was of a relatively subdued purple but of an unmistakable antique *aya* texture.

To call the ancient Noh drama costumes spectacular, with their profusion of gold and their bold designs, is an understatement. Yet those luxurious weaves create an effect of unexpected mystery and subtlety. Although many of the flowers, leaves, phoenixes, and checks favored in these costumes appear to be embroidered, Tawaraya fabrics are always completely woven, and it is the raised portions on the surface that give an illusion of fine needlework. This *Kara-ori*, which produces the effect of lavish embroidery, is a Japanese contribution to the art of weaving, invented by a master weaver of the house of Tawaraya four centuries ago, and is still made. *Kara-ori* (literally, "Chinese weave") was inspired by Chinese brocades of the Sung, Yüan, and Ming dynasties that came to Japan during the Muromachi period, but its technique is purely Japanese. "Japanese craftsmen have always received ideas and techniques from abroad with great enthusiasm, but after imitating, assimilating, adapting, and digesting these foreign influences, the craft produces something that is completely Japanese in flavor. It seems to be a peculiarly Japanese trait to distill what is received from outside, to view it through Japanese eyes, to discard those features that do not fit into our cultural heritage and then, by adding something, to create something that has a real Japanese taste," Kitagawa said, speaking quickly and pointing to specific color and motif to underline his points.

The *kinran* (gold-patterned) brocades on the tatami beside him illustrated his theory. In these fabrics the design in gold is woven by using paper-backed thread of gold leaf in the weft. Originally a secret Chinese weaving technique that the Japanese learned from immigrant weavers in the Sakai weaving colony near Osaka, the Japanese perfected it by making finer threads of better gold to create brocades of true Japanese flavor. *Kinran* brocades are still woven, using advanced techniques, but with motifs, colors, and composition that are Tawaraya innovations.

The great modifiers of Japanese taste have been the tea ceremony, which places emphasis on *wabi*, an elusive quality sometimes defined as natural, austere beauty, and the Noh drama, which places importance on an equally elusive quality, *yugen*, whose definition is mysterious elegance. The delight that Japanese take in the natural and imperfect does not prevent them finding joy in the sumptuous and exquisite. *Wabi* and *yugen* are of supreme importance in Japanese aesthetics and have influenced weavers in their choice of colors and patterns. The aesthetic judgments of generations of noblemen, warlords, and priests, differing as they do in their concepts of beauty, have combined to form what is called Japanese artistic tradition. Under the patronage of the great Hideyoshi Toyotomi, the general whose luxurious Momoyama palace gave the name to an era of peace and whose untutored eye loved lavish colors, the weavers of Nishijin embarked on the production of ever more brilliant, flamboyant brocades. Throughout the Edo period that followed Hideyoshi's rule, they supplied the shogunate, the court, wealthy feudal lords, and the clergy with an increasing variety of fabulous weaves. The merchant class, in its desire to emulate their social superiors, placed orders in Nishijin too, but often found that the shogun's stern sumptuary laws forbade the wearing of brocades ornamented with gold. In trying to circumvent the edicts, the bourgeoisie stimulated the dyeing industry, but the masters of Tawaraya continued to supply the aristocracy, influenced little by the tastes of the merchants' wives until the *obi* changed from a narrow band to a stiff, wide sash towards the end of the eighteenth century.

"What I want to do now is to introduce the best weaves favored by the old aristocracy to the people of today. Sometimes it's a matter of choosing what is appropriate, and other times I must flavor the beauty of textiles of the past to create something to please today's palates," Kitagawa said.

"Although I sat and wove at a loom when I was young, my function now is to design the weave and to program the loom. In the old days, a weaver worked out a design, laid the warp, arranged the harnesses required to pick up certain warp threads, and then did the weaving, using a variety of shuttles for the weft while a harness boy perched on top of the draw-looms and pulled harnesses as the weaver called out the cues. The weaver used foot rods for other harnesses. Now, one man works the loom that has been set up for him. Once I have drawn a design and have it transcribed for the loom, I choose colors and textures of thread, decide on the width and type of loom, devise a combination of weaves and textures, and work out how the design is to be worked. I decide on the number of warp threads, the harnesses and their placement, the type of beater for the weft, and the number of shuttles. The weaving pattern is punched into Jacquard cards that do the 'pulling of the flowers,' as the work of the harness boy was called. Today's weaver has basically little connection with the creation of a design and only weaves according to what is arranged on the loom. Of course, his manual skill and ability to follow the design are essential in producing a fine piece of brocade – I do not underestimate the importance of the skilled fingers of a dedicated weaver."

In Kitagawa's workshop, a few minutes from his home, an orderly chorus of clicks and muffled thumps of half a dozen looms fills the air. Seated on a narrow plank at the front of a wide loom, an elderly man bounced sedately with the spring of his precarious seat as he pushed a foot rod and slipped one shuttle after another across the warp to make a line of weft design. He threw a large shuttle of bright orange thread gracefully across the shed – the opening between threads of the warp – and five smaller shuttles of gold thread were inserted for varying numbers of warp threads. Using a comblike beater attached to the warp, the weaver pounded the weft into place, as a complex series of harnesses, twenty-six in front of him and twenty-two behind, rose and dropped to lift up or lower warp threads in various patterns. A young woman working a narrow loom pulled a bobbin of wet thread from a basin of water and then placed it in a large shuttle and slid it across from right to left before sending an identical shuttle across from left to right. The thread had been wet in order to ensure a good hold and dense weave to stiffen the *ra* destined for an *obi*.

At another loom, a graying weaver was frowning in concentration on a *kinran* brocade. Every other weft thread was paper-backed gold cut slightly longer than the width of the cloth; the weaver threaded this into a long bamboo spatula, which he inserted across the warp from the left only. Kitagawa has refined the traditional *kinran* technique. For ordinary *kinran*, gold leaf is lacquered onto a sheet of Japanese paper, which is then cut into narrow strips to be included in the weft. Kitagawa has modified this by applying the gold leaf to the paper in a pattern, and then cutting the gold pattern in strips. This produces a softer effect and the elusive quality of subtle refinement of what Kitagawa calls *o-wabi* ("great *wabi*").

With a laugh and a wave of his long, thin hands, Kitagawa dismissed the difficulties of constructing a loom for a particularly intricate weave. "The difficult thing is simply to weave something beautiful," he said.

"The composition is all important. So are design, texture, and color. But the most important thing is that one must put one's self into the composition. Techniques cannot bring a composition to life. Despite the disciplines of weaving in the Japanese artistic tradition, the weaver's individuality, his *kokoro* (heart and mind) must be projected into his product. Every craftsman must always keep in mind that what he makes will be judged by its beauty and its usefulness. A weaver weaves a beautiful fabric for a specific purpose – a heavy *obi* that will remain stiff, a soft brocade that adds grace to a Noh actor's movements. He wants to create a beautiful piece of cloth, but it must also fill the need for which it is created to be considered a successful product of a craftsman's efforts. Like food, it must be nourishing and it must be delectable – it must feed the body but it should also give pleasure."

In the matted storage area of his workshop, reels of luminous silks are stacked in a haphazard rainbow. Going to a cabinet, Kitagawa brought out an armful of beautiful brocades. His eyes, his hands, his thoughts jump from one type of material to another, in a hurry to introduce all. "This *kinran* combines an eighth century background weave with a fifteenth century gold thread technique that I adapted and refined this year," Kitagawa said. "The loom uses the Jacquard pattern cards introduced from Europe in the nineteenth century. The result is a brocade that appeals to people today and, in its own way, adds to Japanese tradition. You see," said the aristocrat of Japanese weavers, "I try to choose from the past and then arrange or flavor what I find for the present. There is so much of the past to be shared!"

Midway between the factories of Nagoya and the Grand Shrines of Ise, the city of Suzuka in Mie Prefecture overlooks the Bay of Ise. Ise Province, celebrated in Japanese myth and literature as the "land of the divine wind," was the chosen home of the sun goddess, Amaterasu, and it is to Amaterasu that Ise Shrine is dedicated. Just off Tokaido highway, which climbs the high Suzuka Pass on its way from Edo to Kyoto, the city of Suzuka sprawls across the Ise-Kaido, the route followed by imperial progressions and the Shinto pilgrims, who for centuries have journeyed to worship at the Grand Shrines.

In the small village of Shiroko, an outlying section of Suzuka, Hiroshi Kodama cuts stencils today just as Shiroko craftsmen have produced Ise *katagami* (paper stencils) for centuries. He works in a small downstairs study that adjoins the sitting room of his modest house, on a narrow dead-end street, identified in the village by the majestic Japanese pine tree that grows at its entrance.

Wearing a crisp, light cotton kimono of gray with a small geometric design in white, Kodama discussed his craft.

"It is becoming more and more difficult to be a craftsman these days because it is hard to find the right materials," he said. "The paper I use is becoming scarce and expensive, but only that of good quality will do for my stencils. It must have durability and resilience, and must return to its original dimensions without warping or shrinking when drying."

The paper stencils that Kodama produces, used almost exclusively for silk kimono dyeing, are of a tradition that can be traced back to various eighth century decorating techniques. Textiles and leather of the Nara period show that Japanese dyeing techniques, influenced by those imported from China and India particularly, included wax resist dyeing, tie-dyeing, clamped wood blocks for poured dyes, and cut stencils for brush dyeing. An early type of paper stencil was used in applying dye to the leather garments favored by the warriors of the Heian and Kamakura periods, but, by the Muromachi period, paper stencils (*katagami*) were used to apply paste resist rather than the dye itself to leather and to various fabrics used for kimonos. Many of the minute patterns (*komon*) that decorated leather breastplates and armor lining were revived and adapted in the early Edo period by dyers who had developed an effective dye-resistant rice paste. This they applied to cotton and silk through the paper stencils, then mostly cut in a series of very tiny holes to form patterns. The material was vat-dyed by hand and the pin-prick dots of paste resist were subsequently removed by rinsing the cloth in cold water.

"Most of the designs I cut today are the same as those that were introduced in the late Muromachi and Momoyama periods," Kodama said. "The Ise area has been known for stencil cutting for eight hundred years, but many of our patterns are even older and can be traced back to the eighth century objects in the Shoso-in collection. In the days of the Ashikaga and Tokugawa shogunates, all sorts of *komon* were used to pattern the formal dress of lords' retainers. The particular pattern – concentric circles, interlocking octagonals, stylized waves, paulownia leaves, blossoms, or sharkskin – identified the lord the vassal served, and very convenient they were."

Impetus given the Japanese weaving and dyeing industry by the warlord and patron of the arts, Hideyoshi, at the end of the sixteenth century, led to many improvements in stencil cutting techniques in the Edo period. To the original finely perforated stencils were added those intricately cut with a variety of straight and curved blades. In addition to designing silk garments to be elaborately stencil-dyed for the aristocracy, dyers were called upon to devise ingenious methods of imitating embroidery, fancy silk weaves, gold appliques, and tie-dye for the cotton kimonos of the affluent townspeople, who were forbidden by the shogunate's sumptuary laws to wear any luxurious silken garments. The new decorative patterns called for increasingly complicated stencils, and, as a result, stencil cutters (*katagami-ya*) tended to specialize in specific techniques, passing on their secrets only to their sons. While some cutters learned to cut nine hundred to one thousand holes per three square centimeters using a *kiri* (semicircular bladed auger), others concentrated on curving floral patterns or stripes fashioned with a variety of newly designed knives.

Under the patronage of the Tokugawa lords of Kii (the land encompassing the Kii Peninsula, which includes present-day Mie Prefecture), the merchants who dealt in Ise *katagami* (Ise paper stencils) were given special permission to sell stencils throughout Japan. Since the stencil cutters were strictly controlled and were not allowed to sell their products directly to the dyers, the dealers took control of the stencil market and all its benefits. Particularly after a Kii daimyo became the eighth shogun, ruling Japan from the capital in Edo, stencil peddlers became men of privilege, status, and means. In the days of severely restricted travel, these wholesalers were among the few of the lowly merchant class, which ranked below warrior, farmer, and artisan in the shogunate's rigid four-class social structure, to be allowed to roam throughout Honshu, Kyushu and Shikoku. Because of their familiarity with the land, many stencil peddlers were also supposed to have served as spies in the vast information network established by the Tokugawas and soon acquired privileges far above those extended most merchants. Eighty-seven traveling stencil salesmen were reported to be traversing Japan in 1763, while 187 stencil merchants were registered in Edo alone. Despite their reputation for being high livers and big spenders whose influence far exceeded their legal status, the *katagami* dealers did actually serve the Ise artisans well by distributing Ise *katagami* throughout Japan.

The striped patterns of Suzuka were always favored by the townspeople of Edo, and the *shima-bori* ("stripe cutting") technique, the mastery of which allowed Hiroshi Kodama to be designated a holder of an Intangible Cultural Property in 1955 at the age of forty-two, is generally considered the most difficult of all stencil cutting skills. Incalculable precision and delicacy are required to cut as many as forty-two perfectly straight, clean lines to create twenty stripes within the width of three centimeters, but even more dexterity and control are needed to cut lines that undulate or vary in width down the length of the stencil. Single hair-breadth cutouts and fine, interlocking lines must be cut with meticulous care.

"Although most Ise *katagami-ya* have traditionally specialized in one particular technique, I had to master the tools of all styles of carving during my thirteen years as an apprentice in Tokyo. My father, who specialized in *shima-bori*, taught me his special skills during my boyhood in Ise. He died when I was sixteen, but by then I had served as his full-time apprentice for four years. I have continued the family tradition of stripe designs, but I also mastered *kiri-bori* (auger cutting) for dotted designs, *tsuki-bori* (pushed knife perforation) for curved, pictorial patterns, and *dogu-bori* (perforation by patterned cutters) for overall small patterns. For stripes, I use the *hiki-bori* (pulled knife carving) techniques and *ichimai-zuki* (straight blade perforation)." One of Kodama's pattern books contains brushings of some four hundred precise geometric and graceful graphic designs, which he has cut in the last four years. Among the stripes of every conceivable width and rhythm there are pointillistic mountain and cloud patterns, zigzags, both angular and curved, stylized phoenixes and nightingales, reeds and autumn grasses, blossoms and trees. Some patterns simulate basket weaves, fabric textures and bamboo lattices; others are thin lines bracketing vertical rows of arrowheads, gourds, and bamboo trunks, as well as eellike stream patterns, wood-grain designs, wavering stripes inspired by waterfalls, bamboo leaves, willows, and fine-lined grasses and leaves.

Kodama begins by devising the master pattern, inventing his own variations in rhythm and proportion, although he bases most designs on old patterns. From a strong central theme he composes a variety of tempos, tones, and chords, with different degrees of elaboration and variation within the basic framework.

After working out a pattern guide, a small piece of paper marked with indentations, he marks out the pattern to be cut in the center of the stencil paper, leaving an appropriate margin. "Choosing the correct tools and sharpening them properly is apt to take two or three days, but once the preparations are made I work straight through without stopping except for more tool sharpening. I can cut a simple stripe stencil in about four hours, but others take at least eight or nine hours of concentrated, uninterrupted work. I start right after an early breakfast," Kodama said, "and work without pausing except to sip some tea, until I finish when the afternoon light starts to fail. A large, complicated stencil involving very fine lines or combinations of line undulations and graphics may take as long as three or four weeks of labor. After a day of that kind of tension and physical and mental concentration, I fall into bed and sleep like a log."

In the airy eight-mat room where he works, Kodama seated himself on a cushion in front of his slanting desk placed before a window. He adjusted his posture, donned his spectacles, and inspected the partially cut sheaf of eight brown paper stencils that lay on the desk laced together with twisted paper tied through holes along the edges. After examining several tools, he chose a *kogatana* ("small sword"), a very small spearlike knife, its short, diagonal blade clamped between strips of wood tied together to form the handle. Licking his finger, Kodama moistened a small whetstone and proceeded to sharpen the tiny blade with small quiet strokes for fully two minutes before taking the tool firmly between his right thumb and middle finger, his index finger resting without visible tension on the wooden handle. As he started to cut in the right-hand area of the stencil, his small finger rested lightly on the stencil paper, but his ring finger acted as a pilot, gliding firmly across the paper as he pulled the *kogatana* towards him. To guide the blade, he held a steel ruler down on the paper with his left hand, lining it up along the barely visible indentations marked at the top and bottom of the stencil and drawing the blade along beside it.

"The trick is to keep the blade at exactly the same angle throughout the cut," Kodama said. "If it leans to the right or left or wobbles even a trifle, the stripe will be uneven. I must keep absolutely still, even my head must be held at the identical angle, since one unevenly cut line ruins the design. A bad stroke means a fuzzy stencil, poorly applied resist, and inaccurate dyeing. Only clean cuts assure exact outlines on the finished material." Drawing the miniature dagger firmly along the ruler, Kodama paused to breathe only at the end of the line. Replacing the blade at the top of the slit, he drew it down the cut again, and then once more, before moving the ruler on to the next marking, a mere one millimeter to the left. Thus he cut thirty vertical lines in a width of three centimeters. When the stencil is finished, every other strip is cut at top and bottom, making open stripes through which the resist would be applied. "For this pattern, I am cutting eight stencils at once, each made of two sheets of paper. One strong stroke could be used to cut through all eight stencils, but I think a quiet, calm stroke, repeated three times, each one going deeper into the pile of papers, cuts much more cleanly and smoothly. Three nice, gentle strokes

are accepted quietly by the paper, but if you force the cut, the paper resists," the stencil cutter said. "The *ji-gami* (stencil paper) comes from a maker in Saitama Prefecture who provides paper free of flaws and lumps. I prefer paper that has been seasoned three to fifteen years. In Suzuka, the paper is pasted together with *kaki-shibu* (persimmon tannin), vertically grained sheet on horizontally grained sheet, and dried on a board in the sun. After being stored several years to allow the persimmon juice to cure the paper naturally, the paper becomes a deep copper brown. The juice and paper have become one. Before carving, I split each double-leaved sheet in half, using a bamboo spatula, peeling apart the two sheets that have dried together. By allowing the sheets to grow together once, a grain is created and the split sheets retain a fit that keeps them exactly in position when I stack up eight stencil papers, each split, for carving. Each split stencil paper will be pasted back together after carving and after the insertion of the reinforcing mesh of silk."

The sharp *kogatana* for *hiki-bori* all have diagonal blades but vary in length and width of blade and point. A double-bladed type, the *nijubiki*, is used for curved and straight parallel lines, the cuts sometimes separated by only a thread width. The *ichimai-zuki* ("one-thrust blade," sharpened on both edges to achieve slitlike perforations) range from matchstick blades to one-half the width of a razor blade and are just as sharp. The *hori-kogatana* is a curved, pointed blade that is used to pierce paper placed over a hole in a special workboard.

"This takes a good seven years to learn to sharpen properly. As a young lad, I occasionally would borrow my father's when he was out. When he returned, he could always tell at a glance that I had used it and I would be made to sharpen it for a good two or three hours. Today, I can tell a craftsman by his *kogatana* – his blade shows his carving style, his skill, his sharpening methods, his character and even his build and appearance. Very revealing!" The *kiri* (auger) is held vertically in the right hand and twisted with the left hand to cut a pinprick dot or coin-size hole. *Dogu-bori* blades are shaped as triangles, circles, blossoms, and half moons and are used as perforators.

To create a one-centimeter-wide curving river pattern down the entire length of a twelve-centimeter or twenty-centimeter stencil, Kodama has devised a method of carving the left bank first, leaving certain connecting areas uncut so that the paper will not move when he returns to carve the right river bank; once the whole stencil is cut he returns to cut away the connections, which have kept the stencil firm enough for proper cutting. No further snips take place until the flimsy stencil is anchored to the silk web inserted between the two sheets.

The unique *ito-ire* ("thread insertion") technique serves to strengthen extremely delicately cut stencils and was devised in the mid eighteenth century to support ornately carved designs.

In a drying and storage room, the stencil cutter's wife strings silk threads into a rectangular, patterned web. Hanging above her worktable is a wooden reel wound with twenty-one-denier silk consisting of the three-denier threads of seven cocoons twisted together to form a white thread as fine as that used for stockings. Mrs. Kodama strings the thread on the wooden frame edged with wooden pegs, achieving patterns resembling fine graph paper, or decorative meshes with square or triangular openings, guided by chalk marks made on the pegged frame by her husband.

To insert the web in the stencil, she first places the bottom stencil on a wooden frame that sits on a foundation board. She wets the edges of the stencil with persimmon tannin to paste it to the frame and then moves the framed stencil to the storage room to dry for three hours, after which the taut stencil is placed again on the foundation board, now covered with a wet sheet of paper, which serves to keep the framed stencil from slipping. Mrs. Kodama then brushes the entire stencil with persimmon tannin and lifts the silk mesh onto the wet surface; the mesh's pegged frame fits snugly around the framed stencil. Next comes the difficult process of laying the top stencil over the wet mesh and aligning it perfectly with the bottom stencil by using the four holes cut in the margins of both stencils. More sticky juice is then brushed onto the top stencil, and, with a needle-tipped stick, Mrs. Kodama now adjusts cut portions of the two stencils so they match exactly. She cuts the silk threads by running a razor carefully around the inside of the mesh frame and removes the frame. Then she raises the stencil frame, and slowly peeling off the wet paper underneath, she blows into the stencil to remove the excess persimmon tannin that clogs the cut-out sections. Bubbles and sticky lumps removed, she turns the paired stencils to the right and the left, blowing from each side to lift up and adjust slipped portions of the soggy single stencils so they fit perfectly. The next step is to use the needle-tipped stick to adjust the silk mesh; some threads must be moved to add support to particularly delicate leaves or lines, others pushed apart or pulled together to permit Kodama to do his final snipping of connecting areas on the dry stencil without breaking a thread. The stencil is then dried in the sun for several hours and in the drying racks for a week. Another coating of persimmon tannin, a week more in the shelves, then one or two more coatings and drying periods precede the removal of the dried stencil from the wooden frame. After inspection and final cutting of fine areas by Kodama, the stencil is put away for three years.

"This aging time is very important: the paper, the persimmon tannin, and the silk must grow together to form one unit, a single stencil. This seasoning ensures that the dyeing will proceed well. After all, I am a craftsman, and I'm happy to say that dyers who use my stencils find them sturdy enough to use them for eighty bolts of cloths, which they say dye perfectly despite the intricate patterns. So, you see, it is worth the extra effort. I never know how well I've carved a stencil until I see the dyed material. An expert dyer needs a well-cut stencil to produce a precisely outlined, well-dyed design. Similarly, a stencil can be ruined by a heavy-handed stenciller, and the design weakened by an inexpert dyer. Of course, I don't see the results of my work until almost four years after I've cut the stencil. So I just keep cutting as well as I can."

For fifty-three years, Kodama has dedicated his life to his craft, and his wife learned the silk webbing technique from her mother-in-law as a bride of seventeen. Since Kodama's son has not chosen to follow his father's work, Hiroshi Kodama says he is the last craftsman of his line.

Tatsuaki Kuroda   *Woodworker*   plates 44–49

"What I try to do is to help wood become what it wants to be." Tatsuaki Kuroda's long hands caressed slabs of *keyaki* (zelkova) wood set out in front of his house to dry in the summer Kyoto sun. "When I look at a piece of wood, I envision something beautiful. I try to make a box or a table that will either bring out the natural beauty of the wood or enhance its particular quality of strength or lightness."

The tall cabinetmaker had to stoop as he walked beneath the wisteria arbor framing the entrance of his house and workshop, which borders directly on a narrow street not far from Gion Shrine. In the living room, amid a cosy clutter of antique boxes, baskets, chests, ceramics, and books, Kuroda lowered his long, thin frame to the tatami mats and leaned against a backrest set before a low table.

The youngest of eight children of a successful Kyoto lacquerer, Tatsuaki Kuroda decided as a young boy that he would not be happy working within the confines of the specialized craft followed by his father. The senior Kuroda was classified as a *nuri shi*, a special type of lacquerer whose work was limited to applying basic coats of lacquer to objects before decoration was begun. Young Tatsuaki wanted to become a craftsman whose participation extended beyond the intermediate processes of priming a wooden core, coating it with successive layers of lacquer and polishing it to prepare it for the artistry of the *maki-e shi*, the lacquer artist who decorated and completed the article.

"Watching my father and his twenty apprentices work on the wooden boxes, bowls, and trays that were brought to him for lacquering and then seeing the coated pieces being taken to a lacquer painter or inlayer to be finished, I became determined to master the entire process myself from the basic woodwork to the finished decorated article.

"My father often said that the work of a *nuri shi* was a thankless task, although it had long been traditional in Japan for specialized craftsmen to combine their talents to produce one article. I don't believe in too much specialization in the crafts, as I feel that the quality of the article produced falls to the level of the least skilled worker. Besides, I am too impatient and prefer to make the whole cabinet or tea caddy myself. I believe in a single, continuous process and prefer to be a one-man assembly line." Kuroda spoke with the buoyant air of a young man starting a new and exciting career, although he has spent over half a century in woodwork.

By mastering not only his father's craft but also those of the joiner, the cabinetmaker, the lacquer artist, and the inlayer, Tatsuaki Kuroda has become a uniquely versatile artist in wood. Many of his boxes and cabinets have a warm finish of many layers of transparent lacquer, which displays the unusual grain of the wood. A small, brown ink container is fashioned to draw one's attention to the amusing shape of the burl from which it was made. A sturdy round table, decorated in several colors of lacquer, is a bold affirmation of the strength of the giant trunk from which it was cut. A tiny red lacquer incense box is feather-light and carved to resemble a blossom, the satiny, upturned petals inviting to the touch. The entire surface of a writing box is strewn with inlaid mother-of-pearl.

The decoration that Kuroda applies to his wooden objects is seldom pictorial, since he prefers to concentrate on achieving an interesting surface, a lustrous finish, or an unusually textured ground. One of his specialities is a dense ground of shell inlay completely covering the object. Although he sometimes works with mother-of-pearl inlays using either the milky white *chogai* (nautilus) or *yakogai* (turbo), he is particularly fond of *aogai* work, which employs the iridescent pink-blue-green shell of the abalone. A large, cask-lidded letter box recalls pieces of the Heian period, when mother-of-pearl was a favorite decoration.

Kuroda's treatment of *keyaki* to show its grain to full advantage is likewise inspired by ancient technique. The most famous early example existing in Japan is the handsome Korean style cabinet that was made for the Emperor Temmu in the seventh century and eventually placed in the Shoso-in repository a century later.

Although he uses sprinklings of silver dust, shell inlays, carving, various colored lacquers, and other decorative techniques, Kuroda leaves work in gold to others. "I've worked in gold but I found I didn't enjoy it. I prefer using these other materials. There seems to me to be more room to innovate with them, since so much has already been done in gold lacquer. But I may return to it again later. There are really many things I am eager to try, many, many more." The articles that Kuroda produces today, with the exception of an occasional European type dining set or bookshelf, are all pieces that have traditionally been made by fine woodworkers and lacquer artists since the sixth century. Cabinetmakers and lacquer artists first concentrated on religious articles such as portable shrines, boxes for scriptures and priest robes, and offering tables.

The remarkable collection of articles used by or presented to Emperor Shomu in the eighth century, which is now in the Shoso-in Imperial Repository, includes a great amount of furniture.

Shelved cabinets, storage cabinets, armrests, writing desks, treasure chests, mirror boxes, food containers, and braziers were beautifully finished and decorated for the use of the clergy and court. In the Heian period, boxes of every imaginable size, shape and finish were considered absolutely essential for letters, poems, writing utensils, sutras, incense, cosmetics, combs, clothing, and food; larger decorated boxes served as night tables, traveling containers, picnic baskets, and lampholders. Clothing racks and sword stands, food trays and washstands, sweet dishes, soup bowls, smoking sets, and hand warmers became more and more elaborate as woodworkers and lacquer artists grew in number and advanced in technique. The establishment of the tea ceremony as an important social grace in the Momoyama period heralded the creation of a new category of lacquer articles, of which the *natsume* (tea caddy) remains the most important.

In addition to boxes in endless variety, shelved cabinets, cabinets with doors, standing single-leafed screens, writing desks, large four-legged chests, and clothing trays were made in increasing quantity throughout the Edo period, often to furnish the lavish mansions that the daimyos and retainers were required to maintain in the capital as well as to add to the splendor of their provincial manors. Affluent merchants demanded decorative pieces for their unfurnished houses, although the average city dweller's house was quite bare of furniture except for a smoking set, a brazier, a lantern, and perhaps a metal-fitted cash box. A chest of drawers of *kiri* (paulownia) was a luxury and usually kept behind sliding doors in a cupboard. The bourgeoisie commissioned articles not only to be used for storage and decoration but also as an indication of its rise in status. Although two sleeping platforms do exist in the Shoso-in collection, quilts, stored in the daytime and spread on resilient tatami mats for sleeping, obviated the desire for beds in Japan until they were introduced from the West in the Meiji period. Chairs were introduced from China in the Nara period, but their use for centuries afterward was limited to emperors or high priests, who held audiences or officiated at special ceremonies seated on simple, decorative wooden thrones. Warriors in the field directed operations and discussed battle plans while seated on elaborately decorated folding camp stools, but since the Japanese sit on the matted floor indoors, chairs were rejected as unnecessary and incongruous until recently. Tables and desks, accordingly, have always been low, no more than fifty centimeters high, since they were of course used on the matted floor. Since beds and chairs were not required, Japanese woodworkers were free to concentrate their talents on cabinets, stands, chests, and decorative boxes.

"Of course I try to make each piece beautiful, but it is equally important that it be usable," Kuroda remarked. "By that I mean, it should be a piece with which the owner will enjoy a daily relationship, which he will use with pleasure and with the care owed an object he likes. It should withstand daily use – drawers must open easily, lids must fit well – and so it should be sturdy even if it looks fragile. I hope people use my pieces, not just dust them," he said with a laugh.

Two ground floor workshops open off Kuroda's small living room and are bordered by a lumber storeroom, containing more than one hundred massive pieces. Long natural seasoning is essential, minimally five to ten years. In addition to a great many pieces of his favorite *keyaki*, Kuroda has *sakura* (cherry), *yama-zakura* (wild cherry), *nara* (oak), *tsuge* (boxwood), *sugi* (cedar), and *hinoki* (cypress). He seldom uses pine, persimmon, maple or bamboo and leaves *kiri* (paulownia) to the makers of chests who specialize in that soft wood. "*Keyaki* I find the most interesting medium," the woodworker said. "It has a strong personality, and I never know quite how well it will react or whether it will do what I want it to do. Its dense grain tends to resist most finishes, but *fuki-urushi*, a technique in which raw transparent lacquer is brushed on and wiped off fourteen or even twenty times, brings out *keyaki*'s natural beauty. *Hinoki* is a strong and stable wood, so it is good for the core of articles like tea caddies and small boxes that are to be heavily lacquered and decorated with shell inlays."

Kuroda moved casually amidst the neatly stacked wood, inspecting various pieces in a friendly, intimate fashion. Some appeared to be entire trees with only the branches removed, but others were relatively thick slices of dressed lumber cut vertically or horizontally. "All this lumber is alive," he said. "This three-hundred-year-old piece of *keyaki* was found in a river, and it has changed a great deal since it was brought to me. Dealers in fine woods all over the country keep their eyes open for such interesting pieces. Each of these pieces moves according to its own nature and composition. I get to know each piece intimately as I watch it grow. Lumber is more like an animal than a plant, and every piece has a distinct personality. By the time the wood is fully seasoned, maybe ten or fifteen years, I have a firm idea of what the wood wants to become. My role as a craftsman is to give the wood life, to produce a beautiful object that will be used and cherished."

Kuroda wandered about happily in the cramped workshop, picking up a small plane and remarking on its fine blade, asking his second son to sharpen a chisel, and stroking a large slab of *keyaki* that he said had been cut in northern Japan over five hundred years ago. He had an air of expectant delight about him, and his gentle laugh came often. He patted a large dog that sat quietly wagging its tail at one end of the room, then clucked a greeting to two chipmunks that scampered in a cage. Embracing his little grandson, Kuroda conversed seriously with him about the toy the two-year-old clutched in his hand.

Sitting down on a thin cushion placed in front of a slanting workboard, he adjusted his indigo work jacket to give his long arms freedom. After a careful inspection, he sorted through several small planes before deciding which one to use. With small, delicate strokes, he pulled the plane towards him, giving a very slight curve to the lid of a box and leaving a small pile of wood shavings like a baby's ringlets on the floor. After using several small planes, he reached for a large carpenter's plane.

"I use ordinary carpenter's tools as well as the cabinetmaker's smaller ones," he said. "It is important to know your tools well so that exactly the right stroke or angle can be achieved at each stage. Sometimes it's a bother to fuss over the tools when I'm impatient to get on with what I picture in my mind, but it has to be done."

To create a wooden structure or core, the shape is chiseled out or constructed by gluing pieces of wood together with a lacquer paste. A priming coat of raw, liquid lacquer and a wheat starch (*mugi urushi*) is applied to the joints and flaws. Hemp cloth is affixed using a sticky, lacquer liquid. This *nuno-bari*, or cloth-covering process, is often repeated several times, each layer dried and polished with an abrasive stone. Next come layers of a lacquer and clay compound to create an enveloping undercoat. Each of the five to thirty layers of the thick mixture is applied with a wide, wooden spatula, then dried and polished. Next, coatings of black liquid lacquer (*naka-nuri*) are applied with a broad, flat brush, as are any intermediate layers of colored lacquer and also the final layers of the most refined lacquer. Since every coating of lacquer must be allowed to harden in the *muro* (damp press) before being polished with a stone, a piece of fine charcoal, or a calcified deerhorn before the next coating is applied, even a simple tea caddy may take eight months to complete. The lacquerer must estimate the thickness that the layers of lacquer will attain: to make a box fit perfectly, he must take into account the fact that thirty coatings may add one millimeter to each surface, whereas eighty layers will add three millimeters.

In the four small upstairs rooms of Kuroda's house, the tools in use were those of the lacquer artist rather than the woodworker of the ground floor. There his eldest son, who strongly resembles his father, was polishing the *naka-nuri* of a huge table with a finger-sized stone, and a young apprentice was cleaning sticky black lacquer gum off the blade of a triangular wooden spatula with what looked like a short sword. This *nushiya-bocho* (lacquerer's knife) and the flat *hake* (brush) are the trademarks of the *nuri shi* trade. It was with these tools wrapped in oil cloth and hung from his waist that the *nuri shi* used to wander all over Japan, stopping at a feudal lord's manor, where the refined lacquer would be ready for him to use to decorate a set of tables or to refinish a chest. The knife is used for many processes, including keeping the spatula clean and sharpening its blade. It is also used to sharpen the hair and the enclosing wooden handle of the *hake*. In a tiny room, where Kuroda applies the finest lacquer coatings in dust-free privacy, he brought out several boxes of the *hake* that he uses. He handled the slim, long brushes lovingly, remarking on their age or particular use. Most were between five and ten centimeters in width and varied in length from about six to twenty centimeters. "Each brush encases human hair from the exposed tip to the closed end. The best hair came from our long-haired fishermen," Kuroda commented, "but what with haircuts and hair oil, good, oil-free, long hair is hard to come by today. It's too bad the fishermen nowadays don't grow their hair long, the way some of the young people do," he added with a laugh. "I'm sorry to say that women's hair is not satisfactory for a *hake* because it is thick but weak. These brushes are all a bit different and are used for different grades of lacquer, for different textures, different shapes, and different thicknesses. But this little brush here is my pride," he said, pulling out a slightly battered looking *hake* about the length of his thumb. "We have verified that this brush belonged to Doho Igarashi, the great Kanazawa lacquer artist who was the fifth master of the Igarashi school of lacquer work. He died not quite three hundred years ago. This brush that he used is quite remarkable – it has a wonderful stroke. I can achieve all sorts of finishes with it, and it doesn't seem to be limited to one particular technique or grade of lacquer. This brush is my secret delight. As long as it is carefully rinsed in vegetable oil after each use so the bristles stay soft, it should be good for another two hundred years."

Despite his natural optimism, Kuroda believes that the golden age of Japanese crafts is over, and he regrets the passing of the apprentice system. "The Edo period was a glorious one for the crafts. There was a great demand for fine handmade articles and there were plenty of fine craftsmen and apprentices to produce them. The guild system as well as the protection and patronage of the daimyos and wealthy merchants gave the artisan class security. There was little need to worry about whether their products would sell, and many articles were directly commissioned. The masters and their apprentices could afford to concentrate simply on making beautiful articles. A young apprentice entered the master craftsman's family and learned by watching and working with the man who was at once his boss, teacher, master, and foster-father. The young man was thus trained by actually doing the work, not by studying techniques but by absorbing them. After a certain number of years, say eight or ten, the master encouraged the apprentice to go to work elsewhere to widen his knowledge of techniques and then to return as a senior apprentice or to go out on his own. Industrious young men were trained to become good artisans and finally fine craftsmen, knowing that earning their living was not a worry in their years of apprenticeship. Today's society does not provide this security, and often young people are not patient enough to persevere and to stand the long training and early discipline that is fundamental.

"The traditional craftsman – one who works because he loves his work and knows he is making something useful and beautiful, not because he is intent on becoming rich or famous – is the type of artisan we tried to revive and encourage in the *mingei* (folk art) movement. The late Kenkichi Tomimoto, Kanjiro Kawai, Soetsu Yanagi, as well as Shoji Hamada and I were early and enthusiastic participants in the *mingei* movement, and we continue to hope that the true spirit of the craftsman can be maintained. Once a craft becomes an industry, the intent changes, and the integrity of the product and the role of the individuals involved in its creation are in danger.

"The greatest difficulty in my work? Just existing!" He threw back his head and gave a long, hearty laugh. "Actually, I don't look for difficulties or remember them. In my craft, as in everyday life, problems crop up unexpectedly. If you search for them, you'll keep bumping into them. If you just play ball with everything you have, you will get over the rough spots, treating them as challenges rather than hardships. I see a piece of wood and it has meaning for me. I envision it as a beautiful object I can help create. When I can no longer get excited about what a certain piece of wood wants to be, why, then it will be time for me to stop working."

Gonroku Matsuda *Lacquer Artist – Maki-e*   plates 50–75

A concrete block wall and a sliding wooden gate set Gonroku Matsuda's roomy Japanese house apart from the busy, narrow street on which he lives not far from Tokyo University. Opening the front gate himself, Matsuda was informally hospitable and relaxed as he led the way, just ten steps, to his front door, pausing briefly to examine the branches of several meticulously pruned trees and shrubs. Described by some as a formidable person of unpredictable moods, he warms immediately to evidence of sincere interest and a basic knowledge of Japanese lacquer ware. As Japan's leading traditional lacquer artist, he is famous for his scholarship as well as his dexterity.

In seventy years' work in the field of lacquer, Gonroku Matsuda has combined the training of a craftsman, the ability of an artist, and the intellect of a scholar to become a meticulous and inspired creator of works of art. His remarkable technical virtuosity and artistic originality are as evident in the pieces he creates at the age of seventy-seven as they are in his earlier lacquer.

As a seven-year-old, Gonroku Matsuda started his training in the exacting medium of urushi (lacquer) under the supervision of his older brother.

"By the time I was thirty, I had worked in every traditional lacquer technique of the Edo period," Matsuda said. "My early years as an artisan were in my family's workshop in Kanazawa. Later I studied in the lacquer department of the prefectural technical school and in the Tokyo Art Academy.

"My intellectual curiosity was not really aroused until I was about thirty-three, when a wealthy patron, who was a collector with a discriminating eye, urged me to study lacquer made before 1600. He gave me complete freedom to examine his extensive collection. The important thing was that I could handle the pieces and study them from a craftsman's point of view: how were they constructed? how was the inlay embedded? how many layers of gold dust were used? I found myself becoming more and more impressed with the artistic qualities of these pre-Edo period pieces – the sumptuousness of Momoyama period pieces, the strong sense of design in Muromachi articles, the refined Heian elegance, the honesty and directness of Nara art. I had always thought Edo pieces were beautiful. They are, and they are technically superb, but the older pieces, I think, are generally of far greater artistic value. Of course the great Koetsu (1558–1637) and Korin (1658–1716) produced remarkable pieces in the Edo period, but they were exceptional. They excelled in design and were daring in the way they combined materials. Their originality and boldness were a reaction to the overemphasis on sumptuousness and technique that characterizes most Edo pieces. Also, most articles made in pre-Edo days, although highly decorative, were made not just as ornaments or decorations but to be used daily, joyously and easily. Sutra boxes, clothes chests, saddles, boxes for priest robes, letter boxes, arrows, altars, mirror boxes, saké bottles, tables, writing boxes, trays, game boards, cabinets, and censers – all these were made of lacquer because it lasted. A craftsman's true purpose is, after all, to create something beautiful *and* useful, is it not?" The relaxed scholar, whose national role is that of a custodian and chief adviser for restoration, repair, and documentation of Japan's antique lacquer masterpieces, was enthusiastic and talkative as he discussed his wide research in ancient lacquer techniques. Matsuda spoke quietly, using his hands in slow, precise movements, making his points by careful reiteration.

Bringing out a small box completely covered with decoration in gold, Matsuda explained that he had made this *maki-e* (lacquer ware with designs in gold or silver dust) box over sixty years ago, as a sixteen-year-old lad working in Kanazawa, a city long famous as a center for fine artisans. The elegant traditional design of a grouping of flowers and grasses was executed in *hira maki-e* ("flat *maki-e*"), *taka maki-e* (relief *maki-e*) and *togi-dashi* (*maki-e* lacquer coated, then brought out by burnishing) in gold on a black ground, and it clearly revealed that Gonroku Matsuda had early mastered the numerous intricate techniques required to trap gold powders and gold leaf in sticky lacquer to produce a shimmering work of art. "Technically all right," the master lacquerer commented appraising his early work, "but nothing special."

The basic process needed to create a piece of lacquer is straightforward, but the repetitions, the waiting, and the intricate techniques involved require concentration, care, and patience. A core (*kiji*) is made of wood in the shape of a box, bowl, a tray, etc. After careful shaping and smoothing, the piece is primed and then covered with successive layers of cloth impregnated with a mixture of liquid lacquer and clay. Once the desired shape is attained, layer after layer of lacquer is applied. Throughout the entire process, drying of each coat is followed by polishing. When the desired number of coats has been applied, a final coating of highly refined colored lacquer, usually black, is brushed on. The design is then added in relief, in inlay, in successive layers of gold dust and lacquer and combinations thereof. A final coating of clear lacquer usually precedes the last polishing process. The entire process from core to finished product may involve as many as fifty layers of lacquer in one mixture or another.

The high luster that is finally attained is the result of rubbing, with selected polishing materials, of each layer of lacquer after it has hardened. The list of decorative techniques is long and includes not only dozens of types of design applied in gold and silver but also inlays of shells and semiprecious stones, carving and modelling, coloring, surface texturing and special polishes.

"Properly made, a lacquer article will last almost forever," Matsuda commented. "Just think of those early Han dynasty pieces found in Ch'ang-sha, China, that date back over two thousand years and the first century lacquered baskets and trays from Lo-lang. Some of those pieces, made about nineteen hundred years ago by Chinese craftsmen, were found floating about in flooded Korean caves but they are in remarkably good condition and show great mastery of the medium."

The gummy, smelly, brownish *urushi* liquid that early craftsmen used centuries ago throughout Asia was collected then as it is today by tapping the lac tree (*Rhus vernicifera*). In Japan, the sap drips slowly into small wooden buckets from horizontal incisions made into three- to ten-year-old trees. Lac trees are cultivated, but the sap of wild trees is also used. The six or seven ounces of liquid each tree produces at one tapping is strained, refined, and stored in closed wooden or ceramic containers. The remarkable sap of the lac tree, when applied to leather, paper, basketry, textile, or wood bases, "dries" slowly at temperatures between 20° C and 22° C only in moist air.

Humidity hastens hardening, dry air and cold temperature delay it. With proper drying, a lacquer coating forms a surface of such density and hardness that it is virtually impervious to water, alcohol, acids, and the elements.

Lacquer-coated vessels dating back to the Jomon period have been recovered in Japan and the lacquer paintings on the small seventh century Tamamushi shrine in Horyuji temple are considered the oldest extant in Japan. The condition of the lacquer ware stored in the Shoso-in, the Imperial Repository in Nara, gives little indication that the elaborately decorated pieces were made over twelve hundred years ago.

"I was amazed at the fine condition of those Shoso-in pieces," Matsuda remarked, "and despite my earlier studies, I was quite unprepared for their beauty. When I first held them in my own hands some twenty years ago, I was impressed not only by the beautiful designs and fine workmanship but also by the fact that they were obviously made for use, in court rituals or in religious ceremonies – and they were used. Even today, the boxes close easily and well, the mirrors and the scabbards fit. Remarkable!"

Even before Matsuda had enjoyed a first-hand examination of these Nara period pieces, he had been intrigued enough by the ancient inlay techniques to master them. He is today known for his skill in employing the classical *hyomon* (thin metal design) decorating technique, which involves the embedding of design cutouts of sheet metals, such as gold, silver, etc., in lacquer grounds. Similarly inspired by early *raden* (mother-of-pearl inlay) decoration, Matsuda has produced many pieces unique for the originality with which he adapts Nara period shell motifs. The Heian period saw a great florescence in the use of shell inlay. The eleventh-century Uji Byodoin and Chusonji temple's Konjikido at Hiraizumi, the golden capital of the north whose restoration Matsuda recently completed, both feature lavish use of *raden* architectural ornamentation.

Boxes, furniture, altars, and columns decorated with the milky white *yakogai* shell continued to be produced in the Muromachi and Momoyama periods, despite the growing use of lacquer decorated in pure gold. Shell inlay became increasingly popular in the Edo period after lacquer artist Chobei introduced abalone shell (*awabi*) decorations in about 1620. These were further refined by the Somada family in the late eighteenth century, and Somada work is now a generic term referring to tiny bits of green-blue shells inlaid in black lacquer. Today, Matsuda uses the white *yakogai* and also the blue-green *awabi* shells, the *omugai* (nautilus) and *chogai* (pearl shell) in a variety of inlay and scattering techniques, referred to rather confusingly as either *aogai* ("green shell") or *raden*.

"Most of my pieces combine both metal and shell inlay, encrustation, and sprinkling," Matsuda commented as he placed a large rectangular tabletop on his small round workstand. The piece was decorated with elaborate lacquer designs of abstract clouds, rivers, and mists in sprinklings of gold on a glossy background, here mostly gold, there mostly dense shell scatterings. A shelf for the table was decorated with a design of pine tree branches done in high relief, in green-black against a gold ground as well as in a mixed relief of gold and black against black.

"This process of painting the branches in relief is an unusual one that I devised. It is called *neri-gaki* (paste painting), and I use a special mixture of gold dust and black lacquer.

"The painting requires a delicate pointed brush, and the polishing is difficult, since each pine needle must be done separately."

Matsuda brought out an unusual collection of brushes quite different from the usual painting or writing brush. Most were thin stemmed, the handles almost without exception made of bamboo. The tips are all removable. "I have these brushes all specially made," the artist explained, "so that I can adjust the length of the tips with this twine that binds the tip hairs together and connects them to the handle. The length of the hairs must be varied according to the type of lacquer and the sort of design. The brushes are made of various animal hairs – marten, cat, rat, badger, goat, and horse, among others."

In his tiny workroom, the artist displayed the same calm deliberation, the same considered care that he had in living room conversation. Wearing a long, indigo apron over his silk kimono, he sat cross-legged on the tatami, opening cupboard doors and tool-chest drawers, all within easy reach in the tiny room. Across one end of the room was a built-in *muro* (damp press or "drying" cabinet). Since lacquer hardens only in moist air, the drying cabinet was hung with wet towels, and there were small basins of water on the floor. "Things dry best in the rainy season and the hot, humid summer," the lacquerer pointed out. "Controlling the temperature and humidity in winter is difficult."

Matsuda's studio adjoins a large Japanese living room and garden-viewing veranda, but is well protected from dust with glass windows and double shoji screens that enclose it completely. "I even have two layers of tatami," Matsuda remarked, "because it is so important to keep out dust and moving air. A particle of dust landing in wet lacquer or gold flakes drifting sideways because of a draft can ruin months of work."

Matsuda pointed out the thickness of the lacquer layer, visible at the notches of the tabletop where the legs would be fitted. The coating was well over three millimeters thick. "And there are a few more to come – the final coating and polishing is very important."

Picking up a pencil-thin length of magnolia charcoal, Matsuda proceeded to polish one of the needles in the pine tree design on the tabletop. He held the charcoal lightly, paused to lick the end now and then, and with a delicate, even touch, rubbed away noiselessly at the lacquered pine needle. He leaned close to his work, breathing slowly and lightly as he polished, a look of intense concentration on his remarkably unlined face. After five minutes of silent rubbing, he looked up, blinking slightly, as if he had just returned from another world. Putting the tabletop away, he brought out a black *natsume* (tea caddy) with an unfinished matte surface.

"I apply these dragonfly wings with a method that I worked out. It combines several old techniques of inlay and embedding in a new way. First, I prepare a thin flake of seashell of a good color. I then cut the shell into the shape of the four wings needed for each dragonfly. I paste the cutout shells on good Japanese paper. The amount of paste is very crucial in this process. I then roll up the paper, with the wings attached, starting at one corner, in order to crackle the shells to make them look the way the wings really are – this takes a delicate touch – and then I unroll the paper, hoping not to lose one little tiny piece of the crackled shells. Then I brush a coat of lacquer over the top of the tea caddy and, lifting the paper, turn it upside down onto the wet lacquer. I now moisten the paper from the reverse side to loosen the crackled shell from the paste. Then I remove the damp paper and the dragonfly wings should be in place in the lacquer. Of course, if I lose a bit of shell by breathing too hard or by having used too much paste, the whole piece is ruined. When working in lacquer, a mistake means the end of a piece – there are no corrections or erasures possible." The luminous dragonfly wings, artistically placed on the cover, glistened realistically, not a crackle out of place.

Traditionally, the *maki-e* artist applied only the designs; the undecorated piece was completed by other craftsmen. Although Matsuda prefers to do the whole process himself, and often does, "to be sure that the wood is of the right thickness and shape and to apply the exact number of primings, undercoatings, and layers of transparent lacquer that I want for my designs," he also has cores made under his direct supervision and to his own detailed specifications. Although many types of wood are suitable for the *kiji*, Matsuda usually chooses a high grade of well-seasoned *hinoki* (Japanese cypress), free of resin and knots. All joints or seams are next filled with *kokuso*, a wet, plasterlike primer of liquid *urushi*, rice paste, and pounded hemp. Once the primed core has dried, paper is applied with persimmon tannin. This tannin, brushed on generously, serves to strengthen the wooden core by closing the pores. The next process is *nuno-bari* (covering with cloth) in which a lacquer-rice paste mixture is used to attach pieces of soft hemp cloth over the core to envelop it entirely.

"I do this repeatedly for each piece," the craftsman said, "to build up a strong core on the wooden surface. Each layer must, of course, be dried for several days in the *muro* before the next is attached. The next layers are of lacquer mixed with burned clay, and are applied with a wooden spatula. Several coatings are applied, each dried and smoothed down."

Bringing out a drawer full of flat, rectangular brushes, Matsuda demonstrated the light, smooth stroke required to apply a thin layer of good quality lacquer to the prepared core. The brush is held vertically, and the lacquer floated evenly over the entire surface. "These brushes are unique to Japan," Matsuda explained. "Human hair, of Japanese women, is encased in wood the entire length of the brush. Once the tip gets worn down, I sharpen it, wood and all, with a small knife just as I would a rectangular pencil. These are all made to my taste – various lengths, widths, thicknesses, and different densities of tips, etc. Those with the hair cut diagonally are for brushing liquid lacquer into corners."

Each coating of *urushi* must be dried and polished. As many as thirty base layers may be applied, successive layers using more refined lacquer and polished with progressively finer grained stones or charcoals. The final coating before decoration is the most highly refined colored lacquer.

Matsuda drew out a sheet of Japanese paper on which he had carefully outlined the *maki* (Chinese black pine) branches for the table. He had drawn the design using a regular writing brush and Japanese ink, tracing the lines on the reverse side with white shell powder called *gofun*. "The design is the most important part of my work. I still sketch from nature and do brush drawings every day." He pointed to the small, neat garden. "I

have many types of trees – maples, *maki*, cherry, plum, and others – and several families of birds return here every spring," he commented happily. "After much thinking and sketching, I work out a design. I find I put more of myself into achieving a good design than into translating it into the medium of lacquer."

Matsuda demonstrated how he transfers a sketch onto lacquer by inverting the *gofun* tracing onto the lacquer surface and rubbing the sketch paper briskly. The design is thus transferred in white lines onto the lacquer surface.

In *togi-dashi* and *hira maki-e* work, decoration is achieved by sprinkling, rather densely, powders of gold and silver over a design painted in wet lacquer. An entire flower may be drawn on the surface with a brush dipped in lacquer, or a very fine brush may be used merely to outline the petals. After the lacquer onto which the gold dust has been carefully sifted has dried, the *hira maki-e* design is polished. The lacquering, sprinkling, and polishing cycle is usually repeated at least once, often six to ten times, producing a design only imperceptibly higher than the ground. In *togi-dashi* work, both the ground and the design created by sprinkling – "sowing" – grains of metal dust are given a coat of lacquer (usually black) and then dried, and are then brought to a very high polish. Only the design is then burnished with soft charcoal. This brings out the pattern from beneath the overcoat and allows delicate shadings and effects. Then the entire piece is brought to a high polish. The number of layers of lacquer-embedded metal dust, the fineness of the dusts or grains, the colors, the densities of the scatterings, the combinations in which the layers are built up, as well as the amount and type of polishing determine the reflection of light in the finished product and thus the three-dimensional quality achieved in a flat surface. The *taka-maki-e* (literally, "high *maki-e*"), is built up with a paste of lacquer and charcoal dust before gold leaf or powder, or even gold bits, are applied. Most of Matsuda's work involves a combination of the different processes in which the sprinkling of gold is an essential feature.

"This is gold dust," Matsuda said, carefully opening an intricately folded paper packet. "It comes in fifteen grades, varying from the finest dust (grade one) to one like fine sand (grade fifteen). I apply it with a *tsutsu*, a tube made of bamboo or the shaft of a crane feather with silk gauze pasted across the diagonally cut tip. There are many sizes of tubes and gauze meshes."

Scooping up some fine gold dust with the light, fragile-looking bamboo tube, Matsuda sprinkled it on a lacquered surface, tapping the tube lightly with different fingers of his right hand. "The secret is to hold it lightly and to tap rhythmically and softly. Each finger produces a different type of sown gold. The angle varies the spread. A dense sowing is used for a design of a deer or a tree, for instance. The effect of clouds or mist or hillocks demands a wider scattering. A straight, thin line of grade fifteen is very difficult to drop accurately," Matsuda said softly, barely breathing.

The ground of a design created in lacquer may be plain black lacquer or plain red, less often, green, brown, yellow, etc. Although special textures or surface effects are common, Matsuda tends to prefer the highly polished black gloss or gold ground. Larger flakes or scales of gold or silver, either in minute squares or in irregular leaves, are applied one by one to the wet lacquer ground. All twelve grades of flakes, the largest no more than one millimeter square, are applied with a needle-tipped stick, which Matsuda uses delicately, moistening each flake on his tongue before placing it on the lacquer surface. *Gyobu*, the larger pieces of gold, sometimes reach a size of two square millimeters. Solid gold or silver grounds are applied by scattering the finer dusts very densely with the *tsutsu*.

In the highly polished *kin-ji* (gold ground) or *gin-ji* (silver ground) and the *fundame* (dull gold or silver ground), the metallic dust is applied so densely that it resembles sheet metal.

Drawing out more paper packets, Matsuda explained that the various grades of shell scale, which he shaves, cuts, and shapes himself, are used much as the gold is. "In some designs I'll want a curved outline of shell, so I will cut the shell as I go along, dropping it directly onto the wet lacquer. In others, I spend many hours preparing the shells and choosing the gold before I start decorating the piece." In all methods of decoration, polishing plays a vital role: it is only slow, careful polishing that will bring out the beauty of a shell's color or the luster of gold leaf. A minute area polished delicately with camellia or magnolia charcoal or an entire surface burnished with whetstone, a pumice stone, or a special slatelike black river-stone brings out the beauty of the decoration as it shines the lacquer. The fine polish resulting from rubbing a piece of lacquer with deerhorn powder and seed oil, using the thumb or index finger, requires particular patience and concentration.

"The polishing charcoal and stones are all of different shapes and grains. They become old friends," Matsuda said with a laugh, "as I come to know their shapes, looks, and characters, and appreciate what each one can contribute. The deerhorn powder is usually used in the final stages."

Matsuda is as interested in lacquer of other countries as he is in the various grades of *urushi* available in Japan. "I have learned to identify lacquer from trees grown in Vietnam or Korea, and to distinguish between Laotian and Thai, and North Chinese and South Chinese lacquer. I actually use only Japanese lacquer, tapped from ten-year-old trees during fifty days in July and August by one particular grower. I can depend on the quality he produces and his grades – the sap from the branches is different from the trunk, early drippings differ from later, and he keeps these separate."

Whether discussing wood, shells, gold, silver, or the actual lacquer liquid, Matsuda is completely familiar with the botanical, historical, and artistic qualities of each material. Working in a medium that allows for no error, where a careless sigh or wavering brush, an extra tap of the finger, a hairline crack, or the wrong grade of liquid can destroy a piece on which months of labor have already been lavished, Matsuda approaches his work with the enthusiasm of a creative artist and the quiet confidence of a trained technician.

"The most difficult part of a lacquerer's work is without any doubt the creation of the design. Once I have the design worked out in my head, after weeks or months of thought – once I really have the design – doing it in lacquer is really not too difficult."

Kyuwa Miwa *Potter – Hagi* plates 58–63

Three hundred years ago, ten generations past, Kyusetsu Miwa, a potter, left his home near Nara to settle in the castle town of Hagi in the southern part of the Japan Sea coast of Honshu. Today, his descendant, Kyuwa Miwa X, combines indigenous ceramic traditions with Korean pottery techniques brought to Hagi from the mainland in 1598. Although the great Hideyoshi's Korean campaigns of 1592–93 and 1597–98 were political and military failures, his powerful feudal lords changed the course of Japanese ceramics by returning to Japan with numerous Korean potters. Among the lords who used force or persuasion to transplant Korean potters to Japan was Terumoto Mori whose control of ten of the southernmost provinces of Honshu made him close to the richest and most powerful daimyo in Japan. At the bidding of this great feudal lord, Korean potter Li Kyong, later known by his Japanese name of Koraizaemon, established a kiln in Hagi to produce simple Korean type pottery bowls for use in Lord Mori's tea ceremonies. It was Koraizaemon who laid the foundations for the pottery industry of Hagi in 1598, but it is the Miwa potters who have injected a strong Japanese flavor into the ware produced there.

"The early Japanese tea masters recognized and appreciated the beauty of the simple Korean pottery bowls. The Ido bowls, as we call those early Korean bowls, were adopted for the tea ceremony in the late sixteenth century and inspired many potters. I have studied many Korean pottery traditions but I have also adopted certain characteristics of the Raku potters of Kyoto and the Shino potters of Mino, so my Hagi ware is a result of combining Korean and true Japanese influences. Some potters here still make purely Korean type pottery, but I make pottery in which the Korean and Japanese heritages are fused." Miwa was cheerful and relaxed in gray flannels and a tweed jacket. His home is in the Matsumoto section of Hagi, west of the old Mori castle walls. Beyond his carefully groomed garden rise the hills that enclose the port town of Hagi on three sides. Mrs. Miwa, dressed in kimono, proceeded to serve frothy green tea in large bowls made by her husband. The willow green tea accentuated the soft, loquat-colored clay of one bowl with a thin, semiopaque crackled white glaze; congealed drops of the thick white glaze on the other bowl appeared to be frozen in motion.

"I use only white glazes," Miwa said. "I have done the pinkish glazes and the creamy white ones, but for some years now I have used only white. My glazes are a mixture of feldspar, wood ash, and rice husk ash. There are all sorts of variations possible by adjusting the ratio of these ingredients so that the glazes vary in opacity, luster, and crackle. As the bowls are used for tea, the color changes and enhances the appearance of the distinctive Hagi crackle."

Miwa has worked with the light, soft clay of Hagi since he was sixteen, studying and working with his father, the ninth generation Miwa potter. "My father had me stop school after my second year in middle school because he and my grandfather felt that if a potter starts working with clay after he is twenty, his mind is apt to be advanced but his hands will not do what they are told. I first put my hands into clay over sixty years ago. My father taught me without saying much, but when he was sixty he gave me my name, Kyuwa, and designated me the tenth generation potter of our family and his successor. I was thirty-two at the time, and he turned the kiln over to me, an indication of his confidence in me although he had never spoken of it much. I haven't spent time studying in other kilns. I've spent my whole career in the Miwa kiln here in Hagi."

Hagi ware, along with Raku pottery and Shino ware, has been a favorite with tea devotees for almost four hundred years. Sen-no-Rikyu and Hideyoshi praised and used it often, and Kobori Enshu, also a celebrated tea master, included it in his lists of favorite or recommended kilns. Among its distinctive qualities are a pleasing texture that is not as rough to the touch as Shigaraki or Bizen ware, a texture that varies from eggshell to sharkskin, and a weight that makes even the large tea ceremony bowls sit comfortably in the hand.

"There is a great dearth of clay," Miwa said. "It comes from Bofu, south of here. Actually, we have enough clay to last for another fifty or one hundred years because our family has a tradition of storing clay for a long time. The texture improves with age. I make most of my pieces for tea ceremony – bowls, water containers, tea caddies, dishes for serving food, and so on – and since I don't make very many pieces in one year, there will be plenty of clay for my brother and his sons." Since Miwa has no sons, he recently passed the title of eleventh generation potter of the Miwa family to his younger brother, Kyusetsu, a man in his sixties who has worked at the potter's wheel since the age of twenty-two. Only a few minutes' walk from his elder brother's house, Kyusetsu's compound contains the old family home, a tea ceremony house with gardens and a pond, as well as a five-chambered climbing kiln that had been built by the brothers' grandfather one hundred years ago. It is in this kiln that both Kyuwa and Kyusetsu fire their pots every winter, using pine wood to bring the temperature to just over 1250° C.

Although Miwa used to live and work in the main compound, he now has his foot wheel set up in a small sunny workroom next to his new house. "It takes me a long time to work out exactly the type of bowl to make," Miwa said. "Once I have worked that out in my mind, the work at the wheel does not take too long."

Behind the strong individual imprint in Miwa's pieces are strong echoes of the famous Ido bowl that is now Daitokuji temple's most precious teabowl, named "Kizaemon." Commonplace Korean rice bowls, made by rural craftsmen for farmers' tables, appeared in Japan in the late sixteenth century and immediately captured the interest of the early tea masters. These bowls, roughly fashioned of coarse, porous clay and dipped or rudely swabbed with various glazes or white slip had a vital, simple quality that was in keeping with the tea spirit advocated by Sen-no-Rikyu. Tea devotees soon learned to appreciate the vigorous forms, the broken glaze, and the bare foot rim. These artless creations of anonymous Korean potters won a special place in tea aesthetics and have influenced Japanese taste in ceramics to this day.

The shapes of other pieces by Miwa seem to reflect his admiration for the work of Chojiro (1516–92) and Koetsu (1558–1637), two master potters whose creations in low-fired, lead-glazed Raku ware are unsurpassed. Some of Miwa's water containers, especially those with the very thick, white glaze, show the influence of the Shino kilns. His work generally seems to combine the simplicity of the unconscious artistry of the early Korean potters, the Raku forms and the Shino glazes with the indigenous traditions of Hagi, but it is the hand of Miwa himself that comes through strongly in his pieces. His fusion of several traditions succeeds because of this injection of personal vitality in his work. His forms are simple and the color subdued, since he uses only Hagi clay and limits himself to white feldspar and ash glazes. Design is composed only of the runs or drips of glaze, the imprint of fingers pressing the clay on the wheel, or an occasional mark of a *hera* (bamboo knife), a comb, or other wooden shaping tools.

"Our clay is slightly pinkish because we add dark brick-colored iron clay from Mishima, the island north of here, and some sand to the tan Hagi clay. After I throw the piece on my foot wheel, it must be dried for about a week and trimmed. It then is put in a biscuit kiln to harden at 800° C. I apply the glaze by dipping. This means that I hold the piece by its foot or bottom surface, insert it in a bowl or ceramic pot of glaze up to a certain level, sometimes absolutely horizontally, sometimes at an angle. When I remove the piece, I must decide how much and where I want the glaze to drip or run or fall in droplets. How I turn the piece as I draw it out of the glaze is important," Miwa said, demonstrating the twist of the wrist and the movement of his whole body that he uses in dipping his pottery.

Among his pieces is a covered, cylindrical water container, obviously dipped at an angle, that displays a large triangular area of unglazed clay. A wide trickle of heavy white glaze seems to have stopped naturally halfway down a low, squat vase. A veil of pearly, semitranslucent glaze adds subtlety to a persimmon-colored teabowl. Two naked patches of black-brown clay, which rejected the covering glaze on a saké container, complement the bottle's milk white surface. An incense box has shrugged off all but a few arbitrary splotches of glaze and shows its rough natural base. The bare clay, often roughly turned, the unevenness of the glazes, the cracks, the puddles, the full blisters, all add spontaneity and naturalness to Miwa's forms.

"Since I do not decorate my pottery with designs, the glaze must really work for me. I do not use a brush at all. My work is based on simplicity."

Firing at the Miwa kiln takes forty hours, and the three-day period during which the kiln cools is just as important as the firing of the pieces. Since Miwa fires only once or twice a year, a kiln opening is a momentous occasion. "Of course, I never know exactly how my pieces will turn out until I open the kiln. There are so many things that can happen in the kiln, to the shape as well as the glaze. The nature of the clay, the thickness of the glaze, the position in the kiln, the temperature, the wind – all these affect the pots. But not knowing until the kiln is opened – that's the joy of pottery!"

Akihira Miyairi   *Swordsmith*   plates 64–69

"I was brought up to the clang of the hammer and the wheeze of the bellows. The smell of metal in the forge is in my body. From the time I was a very small boy, I found that the smell of iron heating over the coals and the feel of steel in my hands comforted me. I cannot remember when I did not want to be a swordsmith."

At his smithy in the small village of Sakaki, 120 kilometers northwest of Tokyo, Akihira Miyairi forges swords in the tradition of the great Kamakura swordsmiths of the thirteenth and fourteenth centuries. Since 1938, when as a twenty-five-year-old prodigy he won national acclaim and a prize for a short sword of exquisite beauty and strength, Miyairi has consistently produced blades that recapture the glory of the ancient Japanese sword and assure his place as Japan's leading contemporary swordsmith.

"My grandfather was a swordsmith who turned to making farmers' tools after the Meiji Restoration, and my father made only tools, but I went on to study sword making in Tokyo. The bellows, the forge, the tools, the fusing and tempering processes I use are almost exactly the same as those of seven or eight hundred years ago. I make some swords in the style of Heian period swordsmiths and I have made some twenty swords for the Grand Shrines of Ise in the archaic straight, double-edged style, but most of my models are swords of the Kamakura period. I work in the style of the Soshu-den, one of the five great disciplines of Japanese sword making. I can make swords inspired by various ancient styles and I copy historical swords of different shapes, sizes, tempers, and grains, but I still am not completely satisfied with my *jigane* (basic sword-making iron; forged into thick wafers). The whole secret of making fine swords lies in the *jigane*. How did the great Masamune (1264–1343) make *jigane* of such superb quality? What was the special technique of those Kamakura swordsmiths in producing such fine *jigane* from iron-rich river sand?" With a small puzzled look on his face, Miyairi sat warming his hands at a brazier in his crowded Japanese style living room. Outside the open sliding doors a handsome black rooster strutted through the sunlight followed by his hens; a white peony plant grew near the house. Miyairi spoke quickly and very colloquially. Whether chatting over tea or receiving visitors at his annual sword exhibition, Miyairi has a comfortable, slightly rumpled look about him, his face unshaven and his hair mussed. His small, strong hands are calloused, scarred, irregular. Miyairi, disdainful of the formality and mystique in which Japanese swordsmiths have always revelled, chooses as his favorite headgear a cotton towel tied in a jaunty knot rather than the formal lacquered hat traditionally worn by swordsmiths.

"*Oya-kata* (a respectful term used by apprentices meaning literally, "father person," i.e., the boss) never wears the formal swordsmith's outfit except for photographs," Miyairi's senior assistant confided. "Oh, yes, the hat sometimes for special swords, but only occasionally, and none of those fancy brocades. After all, who can really work at the forge in an outfit like that? *Oya-kata* wears his tattered black cotton *hakama* (a kind of culotte) with lots of holes and patches, and a white cotton vest, just as we apprentices do."

Swordsmiths have always been the aristocrats of Japanese craftsmen, pursuing their art under the patronage of emperors, shoguns, and samurais. Although many swordsmiths were considered mere craftsmen, the most skilled were honored and revered as artists who, through mystical rituals of fire, water, and earth, produced not only beautiful weapons but also magical symbols of power. The cult of the samurai was based on the premise that the sword was the very soul of the warrior, who, without a sword, was not a samurai at all. Representing loyalty to one's overlord and a contempt for death, the sword has historically been an important symbol around which Japanese political and social development has been built.

The sword has been central to the Japanese ethic ever since Susa-no-o, brother of the Sun Goddess Amaterasu, slew an eight-headed dragon at one stroke. Because the killing blade was inferior, the dragon slayer was rewarded by the appearance from the dragon's tail of a superb sword, which he presented to his powerful sister. It is said that with the Three Sacred Treasures signifying imperial rule, the mirror of wisdom, the jewel of ability, and the sword of strength, the Emperor Jimmu established the line on earth from which the present emperor is descended. The sword of the Imperial Regalia at the Grand Shrines of Ise and its palace replica are still of great ceremonial significance.

Regarded not as a sign of aggression but rather as a symbol of peace, loyalty, and honor, a Japanese sword is usually given a name or a title and treated as an heirloom. Treasured for its historical or artistic worth, for its sentimental or intrinsic value, a sword represents purity and symbolizes life undefiled by evil as well as death with honor.

The hard, thin edge, the strong, resilient back, and its unique curve make the Japanese sword a cutting weapon unequalled in the history of the world, a product of the Japanese forging and tempering methods that reached their peak of development in the thirteenth century, one thousand years after iron swords were introduced to Japan from China. Great advances in swordmaking during the Heian period prepared the way for the golden era of the sword under the military dictatorship in Kamakura.

"The Heian period *jigane* was very good, but that of the Kamakura period was superb. The *jigane* used by the Awataguchi swordsmiths in Kyoto, the Yamashiro smiths, the Ko-Bizen smiths — that *jigane* was beautiful, the very best. They could temper it well and achieve fine blades. What we swordsmiths today want to know is how to make that wonderful steel. To be beautiful, a blade must be absolutely clear and the metal must be a pure white color. The fine old blades have an intense clarity, none of that hazy, murky color.

"If the *jigane* is bad, no matter how much effort is put into the forging and tempering, the tempered edge will not be good. I must continue to make better and better *jigane*. From now on, I want to concentrate more on *jigane* extracted from river sand because that is where I think the secret is," Miyairi stated.

"I have been using various types of iron, hard and soft, coarse ore and lumps, scrap iron, and iron from smelters in Shimane Prefecture. Old iron

is the best. Those hinges from the old Daitokuji gate in Kyoto that were melted down in June are fine sixteenth century iron, and that pile of old anchors in front of my smithy may yield some good iron once I discard those produced by modern smelting methods. These are excellent late sixteenth century nails from the White Heron Castle in Himeji. I acquired two tons of old iron when the castle was restored. The old architectural hardware was made of what was then considered inferior iron, as the best was used for swords and tools, but even that old Himeji iron is far superior to the iron of today.

"The old swordsmiths and metal workers knew where to go for good iron-rich river sand, but they did not keep records. True craftsmen don't like to write things down, you know — I don't myself — and any of the ones who did keep records never produced a decent sword. The only thing to do is to keep trying different methods."

Outside the small smithy used by the apprentices were bales of charcoal, stacked high beneath a pomegranate tree heavy with fruit. Brought from Fukushima, the baled charcoal is used to supplement the charcoal that Miyairi and his assistants spend seven weeks each summer making themselves. Both types of charcoal are then cut by hand at the Miyairi smithy into sugar-cube-sized squares for the tempering process and squares half that size for the forging process. Apprentices start out doing yard work and general cleaning up and then spend much of the next five years cutting up charcoal. "It's not as easy as it looks," Miyairi explained, "as the pieces must be the right size, cleanly cut, without cracks or flaws. Charcoal must be cut in great quantities, quickly and without too much dust. I use only pine charcoal, and since I judge the temperature of the fire by the color of the coals or the flame, good charcoal of uniform quality is essential."

In the large, earthen-floored wooden shed that serves as his smithy, Miyairi seated himself on a round straw mat in front of the forge. Assembling flat bits of iron of two varieties, which had been forged and refined in the Miyairi smithy, he wrapped the square pile of *jigane* in a sheet of wet, white *washi* (mulberry bark paper) and then placed the small parcel on a narrow, flat spade made of the same metal; he ladled a watery clay mixture over it, sprinkled it with rice-straw ashes and placed it in the forge. Holding the long spade handle in his right hand, with his left he pumped the wooden bellows box next to the forge. The flames rose as the air blew through the single hole in the heavy stone connecting the forge and the bellows. After heating the iron for about thirty minutes, he withdrew the spade from the forge, placed it with its contents on a small anvil, and pounded the entire mass with a small hammer. At a hammered signal from Miyairi two assistants hurried into the smithy and each picked up a large sledge hammer; at another signal they started pounding the soft metal with big, graceful swings of the hammer, working together in an easy rhythm. The clear tones of the blows rang through the mountain air. At another signal from Miyairi, the assistants put down their sledge hammers and left without a word. Miyairi put the small block of metal back into the forge after sprinkling it with rice-straw ashes piled in front of him and ladling on some more clay water. After about twenty minutes, the assistants were summoned again; this heating and hammering process was repeated seven or eight times before the *oya-kata* was satisfied that the metal had been fused and refined enough to start the folding process.

Miyairi held a large chisel on the glowing metal block while an assistant struck it and then sliced the block almost in two. The metal was then folded with tongs, and returned to the forge. It was soon withdrawn to be hammered thin by the two assistants, the *oya-kata* moving the hot metal a fraction of an inch or sweeping off carbon with a dampened rice-straw whisk. As soon as the metal seemed to have fused sufficiently in the forge, another fold was made. Sometimes folded lengthwise, sometimes across, the process was repeated fifteen or twenty times to make the *kawagane* (metal for the skin of the blade). It is this folding process that serves to purify and to strengthen the metal, and the layers (1,048,576 layers with twenty foldings) produce the interesting grain in the *jihada*, the area between *yakiba* (tempered edge area) and *shinogi* (ridge).

Miyairi always makes the *kawagane* himself, since this very crucial process of forging the steel for the outside of the blade determines the entire character and artistic value of the finished blade. The *shingane*, the softer iron that will serve as the core or backbone of the sword, is often forged by his senior assistant under the master's general supervision and instructions. The *shingane* is forged just as the *kawagane* is, starting with small bits of iron of several types, which are heated, hammered, and eventually folded five to eight times. The folding of the *kawagane* over the *shingane* and the forging of the skin to the core is a delicate process handled only by the master.

The block of layered iron is then hammered by Miyairi into a strip of metal of the required length for the finished blade, varying from less than twenty-five centimeters for a small *tanto* (straight bladed dagger) to some 1.2 meters for the *tachi* style of long curved sword. Once the proper length is achieved, Miyairi gives the steel strip shape and the hint of a curve, before meticulously shaping it by using a traditional *sen* (two-handled scraping knife with a curved blade). This is followed by filing with large, straight metal files. Careful hammering and filing produces a sword of the desired shape, and the swordsmith is then ready to attend to the quality of the edge. After grinding together by hand a special mixture of charcoal, clay, and whetstone powder, and adding water, Miyairi coats the blade with the pastelike mixture. The wet paste, applied with a variety of metal spatulas, is spread thickly on the back, ridge, and *jihada* area of the sword, but thinly on the *yakiba*, in order to ensure that the quenching of the heated blade will harden the cutting edge while leaving the main part of the blade as flexible as before tempering. The pattern Miyairi marks into the thin clay coating along the *yakiba* will show up in the design, color, and grain of the tempered edge. Once the clay mixture has dried, the sword is ready for the crucial tempering. In the dark of night, with black curtains over the windows to keep out any stray moonlight, Miyairi supervises the heating of the forge, using cubes of charcoal prepared by the swordsmith himself. Adjusting the draft, raking the coals for the perfect temperature, moving the blade back and forth over the heat to distribute it correctly from the thin tip to the heavy ridge, Miyairi determines by color the exact temperature of the steel and plunges the white hot blade into a wooden trough of water. This climactic quenching takes less than a minute. The cooled blade is then immediately inspected for flaws, since even a minute flaw renders the blade imperfect and acceptable only as a piece of steel to be remelted. If the application of the clay and the temperature of the water are absolutely suited to the type of steel forged and the particular temperature to which it has been brought, the thin edge of the blade will harden quickly without cracking, the thicker rib slowly. Final adjustments to the curve of the sword are made by hammering it against a block of hot copper. Next follows a preliminary sharpening and polishing on a whetstone, and if the blade is satisfactory. Miyairi adds file marks and peg holes to the tang and carves his name, date, and other appropriate information on it. The sword is then sent to a professional sword polisher, whose painstaking work, using various stones and powders, brings out the beauty of the forged steel and sharpens the hard edge to keenness, once measured by such grim terms as "through three bodies in a single stroke."

"I'm never absolutely sure about a blade until the polisher has worked on it, because occasionally the final polishing will uncover a small flaw. Starting with the *jigane*, the whole process of making a sword allows for no mistakes and no repeats. Yet it is not until the final stage is completed by the sword polisher that I know whether I have succeeded. I do not let a sword leave my control unless it satisfies me. Swords for the emperor and for the Ise Grand Shrines must of course be perfect in every aspect, but I am also determined never to release one of my swords to a collector unless it really satisfies me as well as the collector. Sometimes they get annoyed because they have to wait. In a year, I can only produce about twelve or fifteen satisfactory blades.

"Essential qualities for a swordsmith? Stamina and intuition. Our work is the type of work that is learned by the body. Using a hammer with the proper rhythm and strength cannot be taught. It must be learned. I can tell within the first year of an apprentice's stay with me whether his body has grasped the correct posture, the speed, and the changes in strength required. If he is slow to comprehend this with his body, he has no hope of becoming a good swordsmith. It takes a year to figure out whether a chap can do the work. If I find I'm muttering and nagging at him all year, it's no good. Remember, our work is not done by measuring and talking. The hammering, the forging all the processes are performed by intuition. It's the split-second intuitive decisions to remove the iron from the fire, when and how to bring up the flame, to immerse the blade in the water now – it is these acts of intuition that produce a sword. The swordsmith and his assistants must work together with the same intuition. I don't tell the assistant to hammer harder; he must know it at the same time I know it. One mistaken move and the sword is ruined, whether it is in the location of the fold, the angle of the hammer, or hesitation at the forge. I judge the temperature of the metal by eye and I must know that this steel needs water of a certain degree of coolness. This is all intuition. Experience, yes, repetition, trial and error; but it's *kan* (intuition), it's basically all *kan*. The flame, the color of the steel, the thickness of the clay – I adjust these by *kan*. People say swordsmiths have secret formulas. I think it is *kan*, and this sort of thing can never be explained."

A woman wearing a kimono by Kako Moriguchi wears a work of art. It epitomizes the spirit of Kyoto, Japan's cultural capital, which has traditionally schooled its craftsmen in the disciplines of the past while encouraging the dynamic and innovative contributions of the most talented among them. The elegance and originality of Moriguchi's designs attest both to his creative genius as an artist and to his mastery of dyeing techniques.

"My kimonos are all originals," Moriguchi said. "I never make any two alike. These days I spend most of my time on special orders for which I draw the entire design, spread the paste resist, and brush on the dyes. When I produce kimonos for general sale, my assistants may take over some of the work, but always under my personal supervision. They are drawn and dyed exactly to my specifications. I participate in the entire process of producing a kimono, and the responsibility for the design is solely mine."

Sitting at his wide, low desk, which is the size of a single tatami mat, Moriguchi talked about his craft with quiet animation and understated enthusiasm, peering pleasantly over his glasses as he spoke and occasionally running his small hands through his wavy hair. The serious expression he wore as he worked changed to a friendly smile as he discussed with modesty and a refreshing sense of humor the creation of an elegant kimono.

Moriguchi's studio occupies the entire second story of his large, typically Kyoto style house located on a narrow street not far from Nijo Castle. Across the width of the room from Moriguchi sits his senior assistant and right-hand man, a slim and serious man who sketches Moriguchi's designs on kimonos using the master's small, detailed pattern book as a guide. Five narrow desks line the sides of the other half of the large room. At each one a young man works quietly, the silence broken only by rock music played softly on a transistor radio in the apprentices' corner. To one side is a dye-mixing area, with a skylight set above wood-paneled walls lined with rows of wide, flat tipped brushes, their stained bristles indicating the number of hues used in the Moriguchi workshop.

"My dyeing methods are based on the orthodox *Yuzen* techniques of the Edo period, but I have varied certain procedures, reconstructed secret processes, and added some ideas of my own," Moriguchi explained. "The *maki-nori* ("strewn paste") and *seki-dashi* (a color gradation technique; literally, "dam opening") techniques were not entirely new when I evolved them for use today." The term *Yuzen* today is generally applied to kimonos dyed in many colors. Although its origins are obscured by legend, lost records, and widespread variations and imitation, most authorities agree that *Yuzen* dyeing originated in the colorful Genroku period (1688–1704), when the popularity of multicolored kimonos dyed in free pictorial designs by Yuzensai Miyazaki added the designer's name to the vocabulary of dyeing. Yuzensai's exquisite patterns and detailed designs were drawn on silk with a small stick dipped in paste, a technique believed to have originated in the northern province of Kaga on the Japan Sea coast, where the wealthy feudal lords of the Maeda family were active patrons of the arts, particularly ceramics and textiles. The quality of the paste was such that it could be used to draw very fine lines to outline designs and serve as boundaries between different colors of water-resistant dyes, which could be freely brushed on the material in a variety or orderly progression of hues. The rainbow-hued *Yuzen* kimono answered the hunger of Kyoto's eighteenth-century townspeople for bright colors and extravagant decoration, since embroidery and luxurious silk weaves had been forbidden by sumptuary laws in the middle of the seventeenth century.

Kunihiko Moriguchi, a handsome young man in his early thirties, works in his father's studio. His work displays a firm grasp of his father's *Yuzen* techniques, a wide-ranging knowledge of Japanese art history, and a broad background in European textile design. After training with the senior Moriguchi, the artistic second son of the family studied in Europe and then returned to work with his father, partly as an assistant and partly as an established young designer who produces his own kimonos.

"In discussing my father's work," Kunihiko said, "I think it is very important to keep in mind the place that the kimono has in Japanese life. A kimono is more than a piece of wearing apparel. The cut is always exactly the same, but material and decoration vary. A fine kimono is an adornment more like the jewels and furs worn by a European woman. Although the form of the garment never changes, a custom-made kimono is a couturier gown and also an original work by a creative artist. A splendid kimono is apt to be handed down from one generation to the next, like a painting or a piece of jewelry. Kimonos are not created to satisfy seasonal fads, but are designed as raiment that will contribute to Japan's tradition of beauty."

In 1652, about the time of the first sumptuary laws, some three thousand ladies-in-waiting were dismissed from the shogun's service as an economy measure. These women returned home, taking their elaborate silk kimonos with them. The merchants' wives and moneylenders' daughters saw these courtly garments for the first time. They soon began ordering beautifully woven, highly decorated kimonos of such extravagance that more sumptuary laws had to be issued in the 1680s forbidding embroidery, gold threads, and luxurious weaves for all but the ruling classes. Moreover, the destruction in the great Edo fire of 1657 stimulated the textile industry with a large number of orders. *Yuzen* kimonos, with their sumptuous colors and extravagantly decorative designs achieved by brush-dyeing various silk weaves, answered demands for luxurious looking garments but managed to fall outside the letter of the shogun's laws. Genroku period novelist and social chronicler Saikaku Ihara devotes long passages to descriptions of *Yuzen* kimonos in his tales of pleasure-seeking and seduction. Although many edicts were issued all during the Edo period urging sobriety in dress, *Yuzen* dyeing techniques continued to develop, with variations, in Edo, Kyoto, and in Kaga, and remain the most widely used for silk kimonos today.

Moriguchi's sketches are the first step in the creation of a kimono. "I still sketch often from nature as well as developing ideas that come to mind," he said, showing several books of brush and ink sketches of pine branches, lilies, sparrows, iris, peonies, plovers, and plum blossoms.

"The next step is to draw an entire kimono, filling in the kimono-shaped outline in this pattern book with a complete design, drawing free-hand but to scale. Here are some of this year's rivers — twelve or fifteen variations on this grouping of curves. Here are some pages of *tokusa* (a reed-like grass). I started with a forthright geometric progression and then I played with it. In these, I bunched the grass in several ways, here I drew them diagonally, and here I decorated only one side of the back and one side of the front of the kimono. Here are some wave variations, and these are chrysanthemums, some featuring just the blossoms and others including the whole plant in the design." The designs were drawn in red and black ink within the printed kimono outlines; they were done with meticulous detail, and each had a verve, a rhythm, and lyricism that came through strongly despite the diminutive sketch and the lack of color.

Both abstract and figurative designs showed a striking imaginative ability, and even a quick glance through the pattern books, which Moriguchi fills at the rate of over one thousand designs a year, clearly shows the artistry of a kimono designer on whom imperial princesses, leading matrons, and young brides rely for a uniquely beautiful kimono.

"I like to talk to the lady for whom I am to design a kimono. A short chat will give me an idea of what might suit her and please her, but even without a personal meeting, I must know her age, whether she is married, and what colors she particularly likes or dislikes. Since my kimonos are not seasonal and can be worn for any important occasion, the motif is usually left up to me, unless it is to be worn to some very special affair. I consult my design books — they are not for the eyes of my customers — and usually find a kimono in it that seems appropriate. I may do a variation of a theme I've worked out earlier or I may decide on a completely new design. Next, I choose the type of silk, usually a *chirimen* (crepe) made in the Tango area, north of Kyoto. The roll of undyed, white silk is cut to measurement and stitched together in kimono form. My senior assistant then sketches my design directly onto the garment with a charcoal pencil, following the design I have drawn in detail in the pattern book. We consult constantly on exact proportions, colors we will use, and all other details. We work smoothly, because we have collaborated since we were students. He is the only person who can transcribe my designs perfectly from pattern to garment. After we have agreed on the final design, one of us paints over the charcoal lines using a brush dipped in the juice of a tiny blue wild flower, the *aobana*. Japanese paper is soaked in this indigo-colored juice and then dried. We wet these aromatic squares of paper to produce the blue ink that allows a clear, exact line and has the advantage of washing out completely in water. The kimono with design outlined is now taken apart — the two pieces for sleeves, the two lengths for the back, the four strips that form the overlapping front, and the collar pieces — and each piece is stretched taut on two crisscrossing bamboo ribs. Smaller bamboo ribs are also inserted across the width to keep the cloth perfectly smooth. Holding the bamboo frame from below, I work on the face of the cloth to squeeze on paste or to brush on dye."

Moriguchi picked up a *tsutsugami*, a small metal-tipped paper funnel resembling the pastry tube a cake decorator uses, made of mulberry paper and waterproofed with persimmon tannin. Funnel tips of different sizes are used according to the type of design. Filling the funnel with a rice paste resist (*itome-nori*), he moved it evenly across the piece of silk crepe on which large bamboo leaves had been drawn in blue. Maintaining an even pressure on the funnel with his fingers, Moriguchi drew one fine, even, graceful line after another. "You have to adjust the pressure, height, and angle of the tube according to the texture of the cloth and the fineness of the line you want to achieve," Moriguchi explained, as with delicate control he drew a curving river outline down an entire kimono length in one uninterrupted stroke.

Once the dye-resistant paste has been squeezed over all the blue lines, the material is sprayed or brushed with water to fasten the paste and to remove the traces of *aobana* ink. When it dries, Moriguchi paints dyes within the outlines of the resist, using a variety of flat-tipped brushes, similar to those used in oil painting. The resist serves as a border line, preventing, often by a hair's width, one color of dye from invading an adjoining area. A softer type of resist is used to cover certain portions of the design while surrounding areas are brushed freely with a progression of hues. Sawdust is used to speed drying of this type of paste, since the material must be completely dry before one process can succeed another. All drying takes place indoors on simple racks that hang from the ceiling of the workshop, the time required depending on weather conditions and the consistency of the paste. An intricate dyeing process may require a succession of procedures over the period of six to eight weeks. Once dyeing is completed, the cloth is dried and then steamed to fix the dye. The pieces are then soaked in a large rinsing pool of clear, cold water, where the resist is washed off by hand or with a soft brush in a slow, painstaking process. Custom kimonos are never rinsed in the Kamo River, which even in the Edo period was not clean enough for the finest robes, although it was used by ordinary dyers. The basic cycle of outlining a design area with a resist, painting on the dye with a brush, and then washing out the resist may be repeated many times to produce progressions of color and intricately dyed designs. Once dried, the dyed pieces of material are stitched together in a single roll and given a careful steam sizing treatment to bring all pieces back to uniform width. The material is then ready to be embroidered or to be sewn together into the completed kimono.

One refinement that adds a special quality to Moriguchi's kimonos is his use of *maki-nori*, a granular resist made by drying a special paste of glutinous rice and zinc on bamboo sheaths, where it dries and crackles naturally into grains that can be sifted to produce various grades; *maki-nori* is sprinkled on wet cloth before brushing it with dye. As he finished his explanation, Moriguchi suddenly leaped to his feet, jumped nimbly onto his desk, and then off it onto the tatami. He stepped quickly over to the desk of one of his assistants. The young man was dampening a piece of material with a wide brush before carefully strewing large pinches of gray grains over what appeared to be a small cloud pattern. The grains adhered to the silk as chopped nuts do to a frosted cake. Next to him, another apprentice was examining a strip densely dotted with *maki-nori*. His task was to remove excess grains of resist, one at a time, with a pair of tweezers,

until the desired density was achieved. "This apprentice has been with me for nine years, so he has just acquired the technique and the eye for this job," Moriguchi commented, as the youth scratched and picked at the cloth. "A coating of soy bean broth is brushed on next to fix the resist, and once that dries, I paint the dye over it. When the *maki-nori* is washed out, its granular pattern will remain. I sometimes dye the cloth again or I may add another coating of *maki-nori* of a finer grade and then dye it. All sorts of effects can be achieved. I use *maki-nori* patterned grounds in many of my kimonos to give depth to the design. The irregularity of the grains gives a pleasingly natural effect. It can also be used to create wave or mountain designs. In some cases, I cut out paper maple leaves or cherry blossoms, for instance, place them on the material and then sprinkle on the *maki-nori*. The paper-covered area of the leaf or petal design will be subtly silhouetted when dyed."

Another of Moriguchi's special methods is the *seki-dashi* technique he uses for gradation of color to produce, for example, a beautiful kimono with a colorful medallion design shaded from crimson at the hem to pale rose at the shoulders. "To do this my father used the regular resist and dyeing processes and then covered the entire design with a special resist, leaving only the ground uncovered," Kunihiko explained. "Then with a large brush he shaded the kimono pieces from the hem to the shoulders in one big sweep. It would be impossible to get this uniform overall shading using a small brush to go around the design, but with a large brush he can flood color from hem to neck. Incidentally, it is very important that only one person do the dyeing on any one garment, because brushstrokes vary and cause unevenness. Even for one dyer to keep the same hue is something of a feat."

In addition to his senior assistant and his son, Moriguchi has four apprentices, who have been with him from four months to nine years. "*Sensei* (teacher, master) is challenging to work for because he takes a real interest in our techniques as well as our design ability," said one of the young apprentices. "The first year or so is a bit tough, since the work is mostly cleaning paint dishes and brushes and practicing fine lines with a pointed brush, but this tedious work is necessary to give us the feeling of the work and to develop patience and perseverance. We all live with the Moriguchis. Every Friday *sensei* spends time going over the sketches and designs or samples of our work and makes some comments. While we are working in the studio, he is always patient in showing us the techniques we must acquire. Not only is he a brilliant designer, but he is also a good man." The apprentice spoke with admiration and affection for Moriguchi, with whom he clearly felt very fortunate to be associated. A warm rapport exists between master and apprentices, and is evident in Moriguchi's gentle remarks, his polite requests, and friendly suggestions, with none of the shouted orders sometimes encountered in a master artist's workshop.

In a serene matted sitting room looking out onto a lovely garden, Moriguchi showed some of his creations. They were all dazzlingly beautiful without being flamboyant, luxurious but never overdone, original in design and use of color but never awkward or stilted. The grace of a green and gold river that swept down from a quiet stream on the right shoulder to a rushing torrent at the left front hem was dramatic. The branches of a red plum tree appeared to stretch down to touch the white-blossomed branches that rose from the hem on a gray-blue ground softened with scattered *maki-nori* effect. A graceful, blue maple tree, almost abstract in its execution, spread tenuous branches up the length of a brilliant golden yellow kimono. An unusual off-white kimono featured a design of mandarin ducks, the symbol of conjugal happiness and fidelity. Of the flock of forty birds, each was different and each meticulously depicted. A male and female floating together, a pair accompanied by a duckling, an older lone male, a single young female, and a family grouping of ducks and ducklings formed a pattern of grace. The theme of conjugal bliss was conveyed artistically and unobtrusively. The ground was worked with real gold dust in a way that resembled gold-sprinkled lacquer.

Moriguchi brought out several formal black kimonos that married women wear, with decoration only from the hem to about knee level. A white crane flew against a large gold moon on the front left fold of one, five cranes decorated the hem of another. An unusual plum tree was dyed in black against a gold ground, and a golden-black bamboo cluster was outstanding against sky blue. One exquisite black kimono was bordered with a pink plum blossom design drawn on a white ground. Although many traditional motifs were recognizable, each was handled with the freshness of composition and imaginative use of color that distinguish Moriguchi's work. Embroidery in gold or silver or in colored silk threads added a three-dimensional quality to many of the designs, although in some cases, it was impossible to tell from a distance that embroidery had been used, as when minute white stitches outlining the petals of a chrysanthemum high-lighted portions of the design.

One of Moriguchi's embroiderers, who has spent sixty years at his wooden embroidery frame, explained that designs of flowers and birds are the hardest of all to embroider in a way that achieves balance between realism and artistry. "No one type of stitch is much harder than another," the septuagenarian said, plunging his fine needle into a plum blossom with his right hand and then using his left hand to bring the gold thread into the next stitch. "The challenge is simply to produce beautiful embroidery."

Moriguchi states that dyeing presents some formidable technical problems; in addition to executing a complex series of processes, the concentration on the desired result is being sustained. "But," the artist quietly added, "the most difficult thing is to create a design — and that creation cannot be explained. There is no point in just imitating designs of the past. I do not call that being traditional. Tradition may be defined as inherited patterns of thought, but I believe tradition comes into being when an artist creates something beautiful of his own, when he handles designs, motifs, and colors in his own way and projects his own *kokoro* (heart and mind) into that creation. It is important to imbue one's work with *kokoro*. Unless tradition has a growing, spiritual base, it becomes static imitation. I have been educated in the tradition of Japanese art, but what I create is a product of the present for the future. We must absorb our cultural heritage and then add to it our individual creativity. That is the only way that tradition can be kept as a dynamic, vital force."

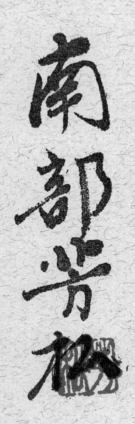

南部芳松

Yoshimatsu Nambu *Stencil Cutter — Floral Designs*   plates 78–81

From the heights of Suzuka Pass, one can see
Smoke rising from the prosperous fires of the villagers of Suzuka.

Wearing the pride of Shiroko — a stencil dyed kimono —
There stands a beautiful girl.
For whom is she waiting?

The famed giant moon of Tsuzumi-ga-ura
Rises over the sea, looking big enough to drink dry the ocean.
Traditional Dance of Suzuka (Suzuka no Odori)

A few minutes from pine-studded strand at Tsuzumi-ga-ura on the Bay of
Ise lie the villages of Jike and Shiroko, outlying sections of the city of
Suzuka. Today, as in the days when palanquin-borne travelers noted that
the citizens of Suzuka were prosperous enough to afford the luxury of rice,
stencil-dyed kimonos are indeed the pride of the area. Some four hundred
stencil cutters work in the two villages producing Ise *katagami* (paper
stencils of Ise) using the traditional techniques of their forebears, whose

50

stencils found their way into the hands of dyers all over Japan, thanks to the persistence of the stencil peddlers of the Edo period.

Too far from the beach to hear the celebrated drumlike pounding of the waves of Tsuzumi-ga-ura above the din of Jike's daytime traffic, master stencil cutter Yoshimatsu Nambu lives in one of the neat wooden houses that alternate along a maze of narrow streets with small gardens, where paper dries on boards propped next to blossoming rose bushes and morning glories. Even at the age of seventy-eight, Nambu plies his hereditary craft and spends each day at his worktable manipulating tiny blades swiftly through a dozen sheets of stiff paper at a time to produce the lacy stencils for which he is famous. Orders pour in from all over the country for his floral designs, and he is known for his swirling patterns that feature butterflies and peonies, bridges over streams of iris, plum blossoms in the snow, chrysanthemums growing along maple-lined streams, and palace coaches from whose windows trail the kimono sleeves of mysterious courtiers. These romantic and literary themes, beloved by generations of Japanese, are used today as they have been for centuries by artists who have adapted and elaborated on them in every medium. Nambu's skill in the medium of paper was recognized in 1955, when he was designated a Living National Treasure for his intricately carved *katagami*. The designs he carves are sometimes sent him by dyers, but more often he makes them by reproducing Edo period stencils in his collection.

"The traditional designs that I carve are still in demand for resist dyeing of silk and cotton kimono materials," the senior craftsman said as he brought out a sheaf of lacquered stencils. "Kimono decoration became very elaborate in the Genroku period (1688–1704). Before that, most of the Ise *katagami* were carved for daimyo, who demanded exclusive designs for their own personal use or for their retainers' outfits; these designs were jealously guarded and could only be used with the daimyo's permission. Such designs were usually *komon* (small patterns), but by the middle of the Edo period, pictorial designs were used more and more for the kimonos of the townspeople."

Nimbly ascending the polished wooden steps of a steep, narrow staircase that adjoined his orderly sitting room, Nambu led the way to his second-story workshop. A pair of wide desks, their tops sloping slightly, stood on the matted floor in front of two large sliding windows. Cabinets and shelves, filled with papers, books, and stencils, lined the other wall of the room.

Nambu introduced a wavy-haired man in his forties working at the corner desk as his eldest son. "We have worked side by side here every day for over twenty-five years. A nice breeze keeps us very comfortable in the summer, although it does blow around the bits of paper we cut out of the stencils." Nambu sat down cross-legged by his desk, turning to pick up a small Japanese pipe that lay on the edge of the large porcelain brazier set between the two tables. His long, wrinkled fingers dwarfed the metal bowl of the pipe as he packed it with half a thimbleful of threadlike tobacco shreds; he puffed contentedly two or three times before emptying it. Then, after carefully wiping his hands, he turned to his desk, put on his glasses, and picked up a knife (*kogatana*) that had a narrow diagonal blade about two centimeters long, the haft of which was bound with twine into a split wooden handle. Turning to a pile of brown stencil papers placed at a slight angle on his desk, he rested his left hand carefully on the upper left-hand corner and drew the *kogatana* towards him with his right hand. The knife raced smoothly around the blossoms in the design, outlining with short, steady strokes the pattern of hair-fine autumn grasses, then whirling around the river depicted below them. He cut with ease and rhythm, pausing only to blow away the snippets of paper that fell from the outline of a tiny chrysanthemum or the delicate spokes of a carriage wheel in the flowery, romantic scene before him.

Stopping for another pipe, Nambu explained that he usually cuts five to ten stencils at once, depending of the intricacy of the design. "This palace coach stencil takes me four days to complete," he added, touching the partially cut paper gently.

"Each sheet of my stencil paper is made of three sheets of this white mulberry bark paper handmade in Gifu Prefecture. Each sheet of paper is well brushed with persimmon tannin, then the sheets of well-soaked paper are spread three at a time on drying boards. The woman who made these stencil papers worked with a quick and steady hand, carefully brushing the three-layered sheets of soggy paper neatly and smoothly onto the long pine boards.

"Her stroke is excellent," Nambu said, "gentle, but strong enough to smooth out any wrinkles or puckers. After they have dried in the sun several hours, the triple-layered sheets are cured in a *kunenjo*, a smokehouse where sawdust is burned to produce thick smoke. The persimmon tannin turns a deep brown, and the paper becomes waterproof and surprisingly tough and durable. In the rainy season, the paper is soft and easy to carve, but in the dry autumn and winter seasons, it becomes a bit stiff and is harder to handle." Smiling continually, Nambu spoke gently and with engaging modesty. His son sometimes joined in on explanations but showed a fond deference towards his father, saying that he still has much to learn from his father despite the twenty-five years they have spent cutting stencils side by side. Although Nambu's own father was not a stencil cutter, other members of his family have practiced the skill for generations, and Nambu spoke of the great joy it gave him to have a son following in his footsteps.

The artist pointed out the lines he had carved to depict a delicate stalk of autumn grass waving in the breeze and showed the minute connecting section he had left to keep the fragile grass design from tearing away.

"When the stencil is finished, I paste it onto plain white paper with flour paste, and then I cut out those little bridges. The stencil next goes to the man who adds the silk backing called *sha*, which must be applied before it can be used in the dyeing process. *Sha* is woven for us by the Nishijin weavers of Kyoto. It is very fine but remarkably strong. A piece of *sha* is laid over the paper-backed stencil and transparent lacquer is applied with a roller. Once the lacquer dries, the paper backing is dampened and carefully removed. The amount of paste I use when putting the stencil on the white paper is consequently very important, because the paper must peel off easily without ruining the stencil."

51

It was the laciness of the ornate stencils created for sumptuous kimonos of the eighteenth and early nineteenth centuries that led to the invention in about 1855 of this reinforcing process using fine silk gauze pasted on top of the stencil with coatings of lacquer.

The use of this supporting mesh made it possible for stencil-cutters to devise ingenious carving techniques for attaching minute dots and hairlines, which were otherwise completely detached from the main body of the stencil. *Kanoko* (literally, "fawn"; word used to describe the spot or "eye" pattern produced by tie-dyeing, which resembles the spotted coat of a young deer) had been favored as an overall design or as an accent since the Nara period, but in the mid-Edo period, the use of *kanoko* for the kimonos of the townspeople was prohibited by an edict pronouncing tie-dyeing an extravagant process. Since wealthy merchants' wives were more insistent than ever on acquiring kimonos featuring the *kanoko* pattern, clever dyers produced materials that were stencilled, not tie-dyed, to imitate the white spots and squares of the forbidden process. A stencil of interlocking square cells was cut, and the *sha* attached. Dots in the correct pattern were pasted to another piece of paper, put in place beneath the silk backing, and then lacquered over. When the paper backing was dampened and removed, the dots remained lacquered in place within the cellular design. *Kanoko*-stencilled kimonos could fool all but the closest observer.

Although Nambu insisted that the delicate process of adding the eye was not all that difficult, his son admitted that he had not yet attempted the entire process himself, since the correct drying periods for both paste and lacquer were learned only after years of experience.

Yoshimatsu Nambu spent over fifty years specializing in *tsuki-bori*, a style of cutting in which the blade is pushed away from the cutter, the index finger of the left hand guiding the knife held in the right; but he now prefers *hiki-bori*, in which a similar knife is drawn towards the cutter. The left hand holds the paper in place, the right hand pulls the knife, and the blade runs smoothly around the design outline. Great control is required to move the blade evenly up and down wave patterns, or around flower petals. The pressure must be even, whether cutting up or down, to the right or the left. "Most of my stencils are used for silk kimonos, but some are used for stencil-dyeing *yukata*, the informal indigo dyed cotton kimonos. Usually stencilled patterns are applied to both sides of good *yukata* material. This is a painstaking process used by a few traditional stencillers. Some large stencils with big designs are carved in pairs and pasted together lengthwise to make a single stencil about one meter long." The paste resist thus can be swiftly applied to the material, since only twelve repeats are required. Nambu, however, prefers to work the detailed, delicate designs of the traditional small stencil applied fifty to one hundred times down the twelve-meter length of material.

"An intricate pattern is more satisfying to carve despite the hardships involved," he said enthusiastically. "The only difficulty in my craft – if you can indeed call it a difficulty – is that while I'm cutting I mustn't let down for a moment. I must concentrate intensely, completely, physically, and mentally," said the old man with an artisan's modest pride. "This is my whole life."

Kotaro Shimizu *Stenciller* plates 82–89

"I simply put patterns on cloth," says Kotaro Shimizu whose Intangible Cultural Property is the artistic skill with which he prepares cotton kimono material for dyeing. The process of applying dye-resistant paste through one or two paper stencils (*katagami*) first to one side of cotton cloth and then to the reverse is by no means an easy one. Dexterity and discrimination must be applied first to the selection of the stencil to be used and then to the placement of the stencil for the eighty to one hundred applications necessary to pattern the twelve-meter-length of cloth for one kimono, which must be perfectly matched on both sides.

Katagami are made of two or three sheets of hand-made mulberry bark paper pasted together with persimmon tannin, which serves to strengthen and waterproof the paper. The intricately cut stencils are further strengthened by the insertion of a cobweblike net of silk thread between the two-sheet type or by the application with a lacquer glue of a fine silk gauze backing to the three-sheet type of stencil. The pattern that appears after the stencilled material is dipped into a series of indigo dye baths has a three-dimensional effect created by the strong contrast of the areas dyed blue and those that remain white under the paste resist.

Brought up in western Tokyo near the pleasure haunts of the Ryogoku and Sumida River areas, Kotaro Shimizu learned his craft from his father after finishing middle school. The elder Shimizu had opened his workshop in the early 1890s, encouraged by a growing demand in the Meiji period for traditionally patterned *yukata*, the unlined kimonos first worn by the townspeople in the mid Edo period. Stencilled garments had been known in Japan from as early as the eighth century but they were usually of silk or leather and made only for the court, the clergy, and the military. The increasingly affluent merchants, artisans, and shopkeepers of the Edo period commissioned weavers and dyers to design cotton garments more eye-catching and more intricately patterned than the silk robes they were forbidden to wear. According to Shimizu, the first Edo *yukata* were *nagaita chugata*, cotton robes stencilled on both sides on long boards (*nagaita*) in medium-sized patterns (*chugata*). Although basic techniques of stencilling using *katagami* were established by the beginning of the Edo period, "long board, medium design" cotton kimonos like those Shimizu creates are not believed to have appeared before the seventh year of Genroku (1695), first in Edo, the capital, and later in Kyoto and Osaka.

Townspeople first wore the light *yukata* as lounging wear, comfortable to slip into at the bathhouse or at home after a relaxing soak. The *yukata* soon became acceptable outside the home when merchants, usurers, store-keepers and artisans donned them when going for a smoke or a gossip in the neighborhood on sultry summer evenings. Actors, courtesans, and town dandies found the unlined robes ideal for nocturnal strolling and pleasure seeking. Even well brought-up young girls, chaperoned by a suitable number of maidservants, found the *yukata* appropriate for *suzumi* (looking for a cool breeze), a pastime indulged in by all ages, along the Sumida or Kamo rivers.

In the late 1700s, the variety of cotton weaves increased, and designs became more intricate – dots and line repeats, stripes and checks, small bird, flower, and wave patterns, landscapes and large graphic motifs, line designs incorporating birds and flowers – all were briefly in vogue. As the wealthy merchant class demanded more refinements, certain types of *yukata* became acceptable daytime and street wear, and, with improved stencilling methods, the *yukata* of the early nineteenth century became luxurious and expensive. Every new volley of edicts from the shogun urging frugality and modesty in dress served only to spur on the stencil designers, cutters, and dyers to higher technical and artistic levels. By the end of the nineteenth century, *nagaita chugata* were so much in demand that over one hundred stencillers were kept busy in Tokyo alone. The peak of popularity for *yukata* dyed on both sides in elegant repeat designs was in the Meiji and Taisho eras, when many fine new stencils were cut but traditional designs using Edo period stencils were equally sought after. The great Kanto earthquake of 1923 forced a sudden decline in the old methods when thousands of stencils were destroyed by fires that broke out in workshops and wholesalers' warehouses. The Shimizus lost hundreds of old stencils they had kept stored in the open loft over their work area. "But my father and I were delighted to find several piles of old *katagami* still safe on shelves," said the stenciller. "We doused them with water and stored them in a makeshift warehouse, a tiny thing about the size of a kennel, which we built in the garden. What a horrible shock a few months later to find that the stencils had all rotted!"

Most stencillers were too discouraged by their losses to continue their work and turned to other crafts, but the Shimizus continued to search for old stencils. Today Kotaro Shimizu has an outstanding collection of Edo, Meiji, and Taisho period *katagami*. He is one of only a handful of remaining craftsmen specializing in hand-stencilling *yukata*, and he is recognized not only for his dexterity but also for his discriminating eye in choosing particularly artistic stencil designs from his large collection.

"I use old stencils almost exclusively," Shimizu said, "as they are generally superior in design and workmanship. I do use some Ise *katagami* of traditional design cut by contemporary stencil makers in Suzuka such as Yoshimatsu Nambu and Hiroshi Kodama, but most of today's stencils are designed for use on silk, not cotton, so I stick to the old ones my father and I have collected in the last fifty years. This one of tiny peonies and butterflies is an Ise *katagami*," said Shimizu, choosing one from a pile of blackened papers, "cut in about 1750. It is made of several sheets of Japanese paper tanned with persimmon juice. I had to replace the reinforcing silk threads. This one of lacy ferns is about seventy-five years old, the silk is the original. This Meiji design featuring three large butterflies is much larger and is faced with silk gauze lacquered to one side. Old, good stencils, used with care, will last for five rolls of cloth, but a ripped stencil must be discarded or a new stencil cut from it. I often give my old ones to museums as a record of old skills."

"Here is a pair of Edo period stencils that I am using to double stencil a roll of what is still called Maoka cotton, although the material is no longer actually made of cotton grown in Tochigi Prefecture."

Wearing the traditional indigo cotton work breeches, matching wraparound jacket held with a cloth sash tied to the side, black *tabi* (cloth socks) and *geta* (wooden clogs), the attire of artisans since the Edo period, Shimizu stepped into his dirt-floored workshop and was suddenly all business. The short, smiling man with friendly, alert eyes continued his explanations in his high but pleasant voice, as he trotted about his work with quick little steps. Adjusting his spectacles, he used a wooden stick to stir a red, sticky mixture in a large, earthenware bowl.

"This paste resist is made of a mixture of cooked, kneaded glutinous rice to which I add uncooked rice bran and powdered lime. I make up a batch every day. The rice I cook every ten days, but the paste must be freshly mixed in order to be applied properly. The ratio of ingredients is varied according to the weather. Every stenciller has his own formula."

Two long, low-slung boards, a pair of fir planks glistening with a patina acquired from fifty years' use, stretched the length of the workshop. Each of these *nagaita*, measuring 6.4 meters long, 45 centimeters wide, and 3 centimeters thick, was supported by three workhorses that raised the board to just above the height of Shimizu's knees. He dipped a wide brush into water and quickly moistened the board, then unrolled half a bolt of plain white cotton in the center of the board; he tied the rolled half firmly to the end of the *nagaita* with a knotted rope, then straightened the material a fraction of a centimeter here and there. To iron out a few wrinkles the material acquired as it adhered to the dampened board, Shimizu used a little block of ebony, an important step, since bumpy cloth means unmatched patterns.

"This is the *omo-gata* (master stencil)," Shimizu commented as he scrubbed old paste from a delicately cut stencil measuring about thirty-six by twenty-four centimeters. "Sometimes two stencils have to be used for complicated patterns. The paper would fall out if those two stencil patterns for the design were combined and cut on one paper.

"About two-thirds of the pattern is scattered on the design of the *omo-gata*; the remaining lines and motifs are cut into the *keshi-gata* (blotting out stencil), which is used to apply a second pattern of resist over the first."

Using a curved, wide wooden spatula, Shimizu placed a mound of red paste on the frame of the master stencil, which measured almost the width of the cloth. Gingerly holding the resist-laden stencil, he walked briskly to the head of the board and dropped the stencil accurately in place across the width of the cloth. He patted two or three dabs of resist through the stencil to anchor it; holding the edge, he applied resist evenly over the entire stencil with the spatula. He then lifted the stencil and moved it down the cloth, carefully aligning the barely visible *okuri-boshi*, the juxtaposition dots that guide the positioning of the stencil for the repeat. Returning for more paste after four or five frames, he completed the length of the board, requiring fifty placements of the stencil, and took about forty-five minutes. He worked calmly, his face relaxed with a look of contented concentration. His compact body moved rhythmically, with the air of someone who knows exactly what he is doing and who likes doing it. When he reached the end of the half roll, he smiled. "No magic," he said, "just care and experience. My father was an artisan, not a scholar or artist, so he never went in for explanations. I learned by watching him, then trying my hand at it without instruction. That was over sixty years ago."

The board with the paste-patterned cloth is moved outside and propped up in the sunlight to dry for several hours. When properly dried, it is stored in the overhead racks in the workroom just above Shimizu's head. The stenciller laughs as tall visitors bump the low-hanging frame, adding, "These were made to fit me."

"To complete the double stencilling process, I apply resist through the second stencil right over the first resist pattern once it has dried. September to May is the best season for stencilling, because humid summer weather delays drying, especially on smoggy days." Shimizu takes a mouthful of water and sprays a fine mist over the *keshi-gata* to dampen it and then spoons on a yellow paste, a resist made of the same basic formula as the first but without the chemical used to color the first stencil's paste red. Using tiny *awase-boshi* (register dots) cut into the pattern as a guide, he placed the second stencil carefully over the dried red pattern, stroking the yellow paste through it. By laying one pattern over another, extremely ornate and minute designs are possible.

When the *keshi-gata* resist has dried, the board is placed cloth side down on the workhorses, and the second half of the material is spread on the board to be stencilled by the identical process. Once the entire roll had been stencilled on one side, the material is peeled off both surfaces of the *nagaita*, rolled, and then laid down, reverse or "wrong" side up, to undergo the same process, except with only yellow paste. Work on the "wrong" side of the *yukata* material is naturally slowed by the necessity of positioning the stencils to coincide perfectly with the dried pattern.

"Because of my age, I now only produce about ten rolls of intricate double-stencilled *yukata* a year. I do about fifty other rolls, using either a single stencil or easy double stencils. I consider a stencil easy if it has large or medium-scale patterns scattered rather than compactly arranged. I think I'll be able to do the easier type until I'm eighty, another five years. I've done stencilling for so long that it just comes naturally," he continued, "but one of the most difficult parts is to concoct a good resist. The paste must of course keep out any trace of dye, and it must take into account weave, pattern, and the weather. You have to learn how much paste to apply. Too little, and the dye will spread, and if the paste is applied with a weak hand, the pattern will show it. You must work with care and you must want to work carefully. I can tell a man's technique by looking at a dyed piece of cloth — the strength he puts into the stroke of his spatula shows right there. If he spreads the paste too forcefully, he will rip the stencil and ruin the cloth. Show me a stencil and I can tell you what kind of a craftsman has used it. A rough stenciller cannot produce fine work. The stencils must be overlapped lengthwise very carefully so that the overlap and repeat connections do not show. Lining up double stencils accurately takes experience and, of course, matching them on the reverse side takes some skill. Another point stencillers must keep in mind is that drying times can only be learned by experience. So much depends on the weather. Dried too long, the paste cracks; too little, the resist leaks."

A completely stencilled roll of material is dried for about a week, rolled loosely, and hung over several wooden rods suspended from the rafters. "After it is well dried, I roll it up and keep it for at least a month before calling the dyer who does all my dyeing. We discuss colors — by that I mean how dark or light or black an indigo I want for each particular bolt, and he does the dyeing in his own workshop."

Yoshida, the master indigo-dyer who does all of Shimizu's work, presides over eight large dye vats, and his wife does most of the preparation of the cloth for dyeing. Soy beans are cooked, ground, and strained to yield a broth that is mixed with a very weak indigo dye and brushed onto the material, which is attached to two nail-studded rods and held taut with twenty needle-pointed bamboo ribs inserted across the width. Entire lengths of material stretched out the full twelve meters festoon the Yoshidas' workyard, where they are dried after the first brushing of bean broth. Rods and ribs are then removed, the cloth is reversed, rehung, and rebrushed with the broth that serves to set the resist. The dried, treated cloth is now strung with fifteen dyeing ribs along one selvage. Folded and hanging by the ribs, it is placed on a rod in a primitive steaming cabinet for ten minutes to increase dye absorption. Holding the steamed cloth by the ribs, the dyer dips one length at a time into the dye contained in square cement dye vats that sit about fifty centimeters off the ground, another one meter buried below. The dyes he uses today are a combination of chemical and plant dyes that are dissolved in water in paste form. Each length of material is put first into a light indigo dye bath for fifty seconds, and then after the excess has dripped off, into a medium shade dye vat. The third bath is the darkest indigo, and the last a light-medium. Twelve bolts can be dyed in something less than two hours. The bolts are then suspended from a bar in a vat of clear well water overnight. Early the following morning, the cloth is transferred to a vat of clean water, where the dyer washes out the paste resist entirely by hand, using no brushes. The more intricate the pattern, the more time-consuming the job. Mrs. Yoshida strings up the material to dry in the sun, and when dried, the cloth is rolled up and returned to Shimizu who, after a meticulous inspection of the entire roll, affixes his seal in red paste dye to the bolt.

"This one came out very well," Shimizu said of a finished roll. "You never know how well you've stencilled until you see the dyed result. I like to look at rolls I did several years ago. I can say honestly that the resist was rather well applied. Now that I'm getting older, I'm afraid I may not be able to continue to work at that level. I have no sons who wish to follow in my footsteps. Careers just aren't the same today, and of course there is less demand for these hand-made *yukata*, for which rather high prices must be charged. People buy mostly machine-printed *yukata*, the kind they can throw into a washing machine. My *yukata* must be washed by hand and never with detergent, and should be dried in the fresh air, not in a machine. If you wash it carefully, a fine *yukata* will be at its best in about three years. It will feel soft but will not cling, the color will be completely fast, and it should last for years. But you must wear it. Don't just keep it!"

Since time immemorial, bamboo has been virtually indispensable to daily life throughout the East. The Japanese feeling for this material goes far beyond its utility. Providing tools, shelter, and nourishment over the ages, bamboo has moved artists, poets, and philosophers to celebrate its resilient strength and natural grace. Japanese children are traditionally told to grow as fast and straight as the bamboo that pushes up through the ground as a tender shoot in the spring and soars to a height of fifteen meters in ten days. Brides are advised to emulate the pliant bamboo, and old people rejoice if they, like bamboo, weather the winds of fortune by bending without breaking in foolish resistance. Tools made of bamboo have influenced the development of every Japanese art. The bamboo-handled brush, the spatula, bobbin, caliper, ruler, and other implements fashioned of bamboo are essential in the work of the painter, calligrapher, potter, weaver, lacquerer, dyer, gardener, and architect. The supple strength of bamboo has provided centuries of metaphor and simile. Its swaying plumage atop the straight stems and the constant movement characteristic of even the most peaceful bamboo grove have been described in court poetry and storytellers' tales, in lyrical Noh dramas and action-packed Kabuki plays. Fairy tales, myths, legends, haiku, and love letters extol the firmly rooted hollow trunk that leans and bends but always springs back straight, and delicate leaves that whisper in the wind, sparkle in the rain, and rustle beneath the snow. The jointed, green shafts and the tracery of the moving leaves have been depicted in textiles, clay, paint, and even metal. A spectrum of black ink tones and an endless variety of brush-strokes are required to convey the qualities of bamboo. In every shade of green and gold, bamboo has been painted on screens, scrolls, and elegant sliding doors in castles and homes. Sparrows, tigers, rain and wind, the constant pine and the courageous plum are its frequent companions in art, accentuating the bamboo's power and the delicacy of its leaves.

"It is the natural beauty of bamboo that I try to capture in my pieces," says Shounsai Shono, whose creativity in this medium makes him a unique artist in a traditional craft. "The special properties of bamboo allow me to fashion it into things that are both useful and beautiful. A craftsman must incorporate utility and beauty in all his products, but I feel function is a secondary criterion. A piece without beauty has no reason to exist. In working with bamboo, I try to approach its unique beauty as it grows in the bamboo grove. Simplicity, flexibility, motion, and strength – these are some of the special qualities that I try to enhance in my pieces."

Shono sat at a low table in the small, matted sitting room adjoining his studio, one of a cluster of artistically grouped buildings in his compound just outside Beppu, the Kyushu resort town that is also known as the center of Japan's bamboo-ware industry. A calligraphic scroll by the Zen artist Sengai hung in the *tokonoma* (alcove) behind a bold spherical bamboo sculpture, and in the next alcove, a delicately woven flower basket contained a single chrysanthemum and some greenery. "Lover of green bamboo" was carved in a wooden plaque over the doorway. A colorful painting by the contemporary artist Shiko Munakata smiled down enigmatically. The bamboo artist presided over an informal serving of tea, using a black-lacquered, woven bamboo box made in Ming China. Shono's strong, square hands handled the delicate white porcelain cups lightly. He spoke informally, but his gaze was direct, his language scholarly. His serious expression changed with frequent quizzical smiles and occasional quick, rich laughter. Sixty-eight years old now, this vigorous man took up the traditional bamboo craft almost half a century ago because he was considered too sickly to pursue anything but a sedentary vocation. After less than two years' apprenticeship with Beppu's master bamboo craftsman, the twenty-two-year-old Shono established his present workshop.

"Bamboo is a natural thing. Each piece of bamboo is unique," Shono commented. "I try to bring out the individuality of the particular piece I am working with to create a work that befits its character. It is not the scale or size of the bamboo that counts, but the qualities of the particular piece. That intricate, finely woven basket, for instance, gives an impression of flickering delicacy, but this round sculpture of wide, thick strips of black bamboo conveys dynamic strength and boldness. I enjoy working in both styles. The coarser weave is perhaps more taxing physically, but once I decide on a certain form and style, I just go ahead and make the piece without worrying about the technique required to achieve the result I want. The three-dimensional massiveness of the sphere is important; however, I do not use it as a trick, but simply as a way of emphasizing the qualities of bamboo. Touch it, feel it, caress it. Bamboo has a natural, palpable beauty that must always be considered." Shono ran his hands over the sculpture. "A craftsman has produced nothing of artistic value unless his work has the ability to excite you to touch it. A piece should transfix you completely and indefinitely. Not only your eyes but your hands will be totally captivated. How could you call that coarsely woven piece of mine a thing of beauty if it were unpleasant to touch?"

Shono poured another tiny cup of tea and then closed the Chinese box. "The last time my friend Yasunari Kawabata, the novelist, was here, we had a long discussion over tea. I put the utensils away and closed this box. Kawabata stroked the box carefully, slowly, and then sighed deeply. Now this enjoyment is what I am talking about. The feel of this beautiful, old, lacquered weave satisfies a certain type of hunger we humans have."

Shono's bare workroom looked out upon a Japanese garden that gave the illusion of a complete mountain landscape. A simple piece of latticework woven from ten strips of bamboo sat soaking in a three-hundred-year-old Chinese porcelain water basin. Putting a dark apron over his homespun kimono of blue and black silk, Shono seated himself cross-legged on a cushion on the floor. He removed the woven piece from the water, flicked it dry, and laid it aside before beginning to work on several three-meter strips of bamboo curled loosely on the floor. Using a diagonal-bladed knife, he smoothed the inside surface of the long strip, first working on short sections, then sweeping down the full length of the strip in a single, smooth movement to produce one, unbroken, paper-thin shaving. Next he split the strip in two, using a straight-bladed knife that was actually an old sword cut down and given a square tip. To remove the inner "meat," Shono split the bamboo again parallel to the skin, and, holding the skin in his teeth, ripped away the bottom part. In a few minutes, he had prepared half a dozen such strips, which, still quivering, slapped lightly against the polished cypress floor of the studio. Picking up the latticed piece, he began weaving the thin strips into it. The basket started to take shape, and the strips clicked and snapped with the weaver's quick, sure movements. He prepared some shorter, thicker pieces of bamboo to reinforce corners and then to weave a seemingly random design into the sides of the basket. He worked rhythmically, his strong fingers guiding the strips in the intricate pattern so swiftly that it was hard to follow.

"I have done a great deal of research on seasoning bamboo and have devised some methods of my own. I use mostly *madake* (green bamboo), and some *kuro-chiku* (black bamboo) from Kyoto, some of it mottled. I choose the *madake* carefully in my bamboo grove on the hill across the river in front of my house, and cut it in November. The bamboo should be about three to four years old and is usually about eight centimeters in diameter. You know its girth will never exceed the circumference of the shoot that pushes through the earth in the first few days of growth above ground. For three months after cutting, the culm is seasoned in the shade. Next, *abura nuki* (oil removal) takes place. I have special equipment that subjects the bamboo to extremely low heat for a brief time to remove the chlorophyl and oil. This whitens it. The bamboo is next dried in the sunlight and then stored in my cool storehouse, where temperature and humidity are carefully controlled. When I think the piece is perfectly seasoned, it is ready to be worked, although of course I keep many pieces, mostly in six-meter lengths, for several years in my warehouse. By the time the piece is well seasoned, I know it intimately – the length between joints, its thickness, its color, and grain, so that when I get an idea worked out in my mind for a certain piece, I know just which piece of bamboo will be appropriate. Of course sometimes the nature of a particular length of bamboo will inspire me to create a certain type of piece – it works both ways, often together."

Although Shono does some sketches, he works out most designs in his head, creating a detailed "negative," as he puts it, to guide him. "This is what takes the time and the real effort," he said. "It is vital that the mouth or the lip, which is actually the ending or binding off, be firmly in mind before I start work. I must decide on it when I work out the base or foundation. Some pieces in exhibits of bamboo work have weak mouths, no ending. That is like not planning the front door before building a house or like composing a song that does not have an ending – it just stops in mid note or fades away. Someone who makes something like that has no idea of form.

"I feel that the pieces I make must have musical qualities – changes in rhythm, a series of climaxes, and an overall harmony. Bamboo works of art must also have an architectural quality starting with a foundation, a balance of weight and form, and reinforcements that please the eye and add structural strength."

The basket form in Shono's hands then seemed to reach a crescendo. He inserted strong pieces of bamboo in the corners of the basket. Pulling here and pushing there, he tested the structure and examined the partially completed basket from every angle. "Even a flower basket has a sculptural quality. I work as a sculptor with bamboo but try to make sure that the material is used naturally and not forced or distorted."

Shono brought out a simple, cylindrical vase fashioned from one joint of bamboo and open at the top where the division between chambers had been removed; there was also an opening cut partway down the joint. "Every piece of bamboo has a front and a back and a face. In the face of this piece I cut an opening inspired by my concept of Noh masks. This is a very basic vase, very sparse, you may say, and its creation consisted merely in choosing the right bamboo, removing the node at the top and then sawing out the opening very quietly. I did not even rub down or sandpaper the marks made by the teeth of the saw. This type of creation not only accentuates the natural virtues of bamboo but also reflects the spirit of the maker. Any disorder in the heart and mind of the creator will show up right away. I can only do this type of bamboo work when I am feeling quite at peace. In a long composition, one can hide one's defects with technique, but in a short, single sentence, it is hard to cover up one's faults.

"Bamboo presents difficulties for the viewer as well as the maker. This rather elaborately woven, round basket is perhaps easier to understand and easier to create, like a long poem. It is more difficult to express oneself tersely. One short haiku contains so much that it is often hard to understand and impossible to explain."

Shono called to his son, who was working in the next room preparing bamboo, to bring certain pieces. Above the snap and rustle of the bamboo being woven was the sound of large carp splashing in the pool below the workshop. Butterflies, dragonflies, and sparrows flew about in the garden, which included a small bamboo grove.

"My *deshi* (apprentices) start working with bamboo only after they have learned to do cleaning up. They must learn to take care of the garden, the workshop, and the house, conscientiously and without any supervision from me. This gives them time to put themselves in order too. They must learn to decide on their own to pull this weed and to let that blade of grass grow. In this way they develop judgment and confidence. Only someone capable of making judgments can ever hope to attain the highest level of true artists. A craftsman who is unsure or disordered cannot do good work. He will never grow beyond being merely a workman."

The basket Shono was making was in the style of Sozen, a tea master of old, but the weave was original. "I think it is important to maintain the spirit of the early tea masters, but I am critical of certain aspects of the tea cult of today. The heart of the real tea spirit must be kept, for it is very precious. We must not revolt against old ideas just because they are old, but similarly, we must not support their defects just because of their age. Just guarding ancient traditions is not creative. In my work, I try to create things that incorporate the good qualities of what is old and traditional but within the framework of the era in which we live. Although there are dangers inherent in creation, without it there can be no growth. An artist who does not grow is not an artist. I try to fuse what I have learned of the past with the spirit of today. I do not believe we should scorn tradition by allowing individual creativity to run wild. Individualism should not separate itself at too great a distance from tradition but neither should it allow itself to be stifled by tradition. One of the reasons I am so interested in the art of other eras and other countries, especially in Kamakura period art and in Sung and Ming porcelains, is that I believe that beautiful, old things nurture the craftsman. We learn from beauty of other times, other areas. Old things, good things, are nourishment for the heart and give the craftsman goals and motivation. An artist must have this broad appreciation of the good, the beautiful. Without this education of eye and spirit, a workman will never become a true artist. Old porcelains, old textiles, things like my Ming tea box, and calligraphy by Sengai – the strong qualities of these beautiful things influence me and serve as an inspiration to my working in bamboo. It may sound greedy, but I think it is very important to steal, to snatch, to take hold of anything beautiful to make it part of oneself, for thus one grows as a craftsman and a true artist rather than remaining just a workman or an imitator of one's teacher."

With a few twists of three long strips of bamboo, Shono inserted a graceful handle, and suddenly the basket was complete. The piece was flawlessly proportioned, the form forthright, the texture interesting. Rhythmical, architectural, sculptural, the basket had been created to be examined and touched; flowers were not required to complete it. Shono laid his tools neatly in the dark rosewood tray behind him and rolled up the shavings, leaving the workroom as orderly as it was when he entered.

In the sitting room Shono sipped a cup of tea as a breeze from the Bay of Beppu dried the perspiration covering his face. He had worked either in silence or talking or humming softly, but now his glistening face was indicative of the exertion required.

Japanese bamboo art combines ancient indigenous traditions with later foreign influences. It was Korean and Chinese emigrant craftsmen who from at least the third century brought bamboo weaving techniques from the continent. The influx of craftsmen that accompanied the introduction of Buddhism into Japan from Korea in 552 further advanced the Japanese techniques. By the eighth century, bamboo artistry was very sophisticated, as evidenced by the examples that remain in the imperial collection of the Shoso-in. Few of the decorative baskets, everyday utensils, containers or boxes of subsequent periods have survived.

It was not until the sixteenth century tea master, Sen-no-Rikyu, pointed out the elegant plainness and quiet beauty inherent in bamboo articles that the medium acquired a recognized place in the arts of Japan. Tea, whose history is connected with that of bamboo, had first become popular among twelfth-century Zen priests, and later it was taken up by the nobility as a pleasant beverage and as an excuse for entertaining. It was his reaction against the ornate artificiality of tea-drinking affairs, against the imported Sung and Ming porcelains and other elaborate utensils, that made Sen-no-Rikyu proclaim his preference for simple pottery and bamboo. The influence of his taste and the social changes of the time served to free many of Japan's crafts from narrow confines. By the early 1600s, the tea aesthetic had assumed a permanent role in Japan.

As the Edo period progressed, influential feudal lords and increasingly affluent merchants enjoyed exhibiting their power and wealth by building elegant mansions, furnishing them with beautifully crafted decorations, and demonstrating their interest in the tea ceremony and Noh dramas. Craftsmen grew in numbers and skill, and their techniques multiplied as they sought to keep up with the increasing demand for their products. Even articles made for everyday use in ordinary homes benefited from this development in the applied arts. At the same time, much of the vigor of the tea aesthetic was lost and became formula. More uses were found for bamboo, yet its development as an artistic medium was limited by the rules laid down by increasing numbers of tea and flower arrangement teachers.

"I have broken away from some of the regulations of the tea and flower cults, preferring to maintain the traditional spirit of these disciplines without allowing them to smother creativity," Shono said. "By demanding a certain type of teabowl, a specific style of lacquer tea caddy, or a particular bamboo basket form, the tea masters established hereditary crafts. This meant that an untalented son of a designated master potter, for instance, could continue his father's tradition, imitating it, perhaps badly, and not adding anything creative to it. This is bad, I think, and has resulted in certain artistic distortions, sterility, and lack of inspiration. Tradition must serve to inspire and motivate us but it must not master us. A craftsman who works within the strict confines of a particular style will not grow. He must learn from the creations of others and synthesize these influences within himself. Until he can appreciate a good piece by the way it feels in his hands, he will never be a good craftsman, no matter how advanced he is technically. The past must be his teacher and his inspiration. The texture, the weight, the grain, the curve, the smoothness of a basket or a pot must speak to him. If he does not hear this voice, he is not an artist. Unless the piece he makes speaks to the heart, it is an object of no value."

Plate captions

1 A stack of paper in Eishiro Abe's house.
2–3 Abe prepares to invert the *su* (bamboo screen), to which a freshly laid sheet of paper adheres, onto a stack of similar sheets. The *su* then will be peeled away. The new paper contains a scattering of colored paper strips.
4–7 Paper making.
8–9 Abe adjusts a drying board. These sheets of *mitsumata* paper will be cut for use as visiting cards.
10–11 Mrs. Chiba in her hemp field.
12–13 Hands of Ayano Chiba.
14–15 Mrs. Chiba at work.
16 Mrs. Chiba at her loom before laying the warp.
17 Mrs. Chiba stencils each bolt of her indigo-dyed hemp with her crest and name as well as "Designated as the Holder of an Intangible Cultural Property."
18 Kei Fujiwara.
19 Bizen pot by Fujiwara.
20–21 Unfired Bizen pots by Fujiwara.
22–23 Shoji Hamada applying overglaze enamels.
24 Hamada's small kiln during firing.
25 Closeup of a vase by Hamada.
26–27 Hamada choosing pots for an exhibition.
28 Heiro Kitagawa.
29 Samples of ancient fabrics (below) and a reproduction by Kitagawa.
30–31 Color pattern diagram and finished material by Kitagawa.
32–33 A silk brocade loom with complex harnesses in front of and behind a Tawaraya weaver and Jacquard cards (right).
34–35 A silk brocade with snowy pine pattern.
36–37 Hiroshi Kodama.
38 Stripe pattern stencil reinforced by diagonal and horizontal silk threads sandwiched between two stencil papers.
39 Cut portion of stripe pattern stencils and *kogatana* (knife). The stack of eight stencils is secured with twisted paper strips (right and bottom).
40 Kodama at work.
41 *Ito-ire* – laying and insertion of silk mesh.

42–43 One of Kodama's stencil pattern books.
44–45 Tatsuaki Kuroda in his wood storeroom.
46 Kuroda's smallest planes.
47 *Keyaki* (zelkova) wood box by Kuroda.
48–49 Box (top view) with abalone inlay by Kuroda.
50 Gonroku Matsuda polishing a lacquered table leg.
51 Matsuda holding a piece of charcoal for polishing lacquer.
52 Matsuda at work.
53 Tsutsu.
54–55 Matsuda sprinkling gold dust with a bamboo *tsutsu*.
56 Vase by Matsuda.
57 Table (detail) by Matsuda in the stage before final polishings.
58 Kyuwa Miwa.
59 Teabowl by Miwa.
60–61 Detail of pot by Miwa.
62–63 Water container by Miwa.
64 Akihira Miyairi operating forge bellows.
65 Two apprentices hammer metal held by Miyairi.
66–67 Miyairi at work.
68–69 Sword by Miyairi showing tip, *shinogi* (ridge), and *yakiba* (edge area below wavy temper line).
70 Kako Moriguchi.
71 *Maki-nori* technique. From left to right, the samples show five stages of dyeing and progressively denser applications of *maki-nori*. The panel at right shows material after final dyeing and removal of *maki-nori*.
72 Moriguchi at work.
73 Moriguchi's assistants.
74–75 Moriguchi applying fine lines of paste resist with a *tsutsugami* (paper funnel).
76 Kimono (detail) by Moriguchi with gold embroidery.
77 Formal kimono by Moriguchi displayed on rack (detail at left).
78 Yoshimatsu Nambu.
79 Stencil by Nambu showing lacquered *sha* (silk gauze) backing. Detail at right is closeup of *kanoko* pattern, which simulates tie-dyeing.
80–81 Nambu at work.
82–83 Kotaro Shimizu applying paste resist through master stencil.
84 Paste resist pattern after removal of master stencil.
85 Final paste resist pattern after removal of secondary stencil. To clarify the design for the photograph, only red paste was used.
86–87 Dyeing cotton for *yukata*.
88–89 Two examples of *yukata* material stencilled by Shimizu.
90–91 Shounsai Shono holding bamboo flower container. To the right of the artist is the antique Chinese water basin in which fine bamboo strips are soaking.
92–93 Closeup of bamboo strips in antique Chinese basin.
94–95 Bamboo and wild vine.
96 Basket (detail) by Shono.

EISHIRO ABE PAPERMAKER (GAMPISHI)

安部栄四郎 雁皮紙

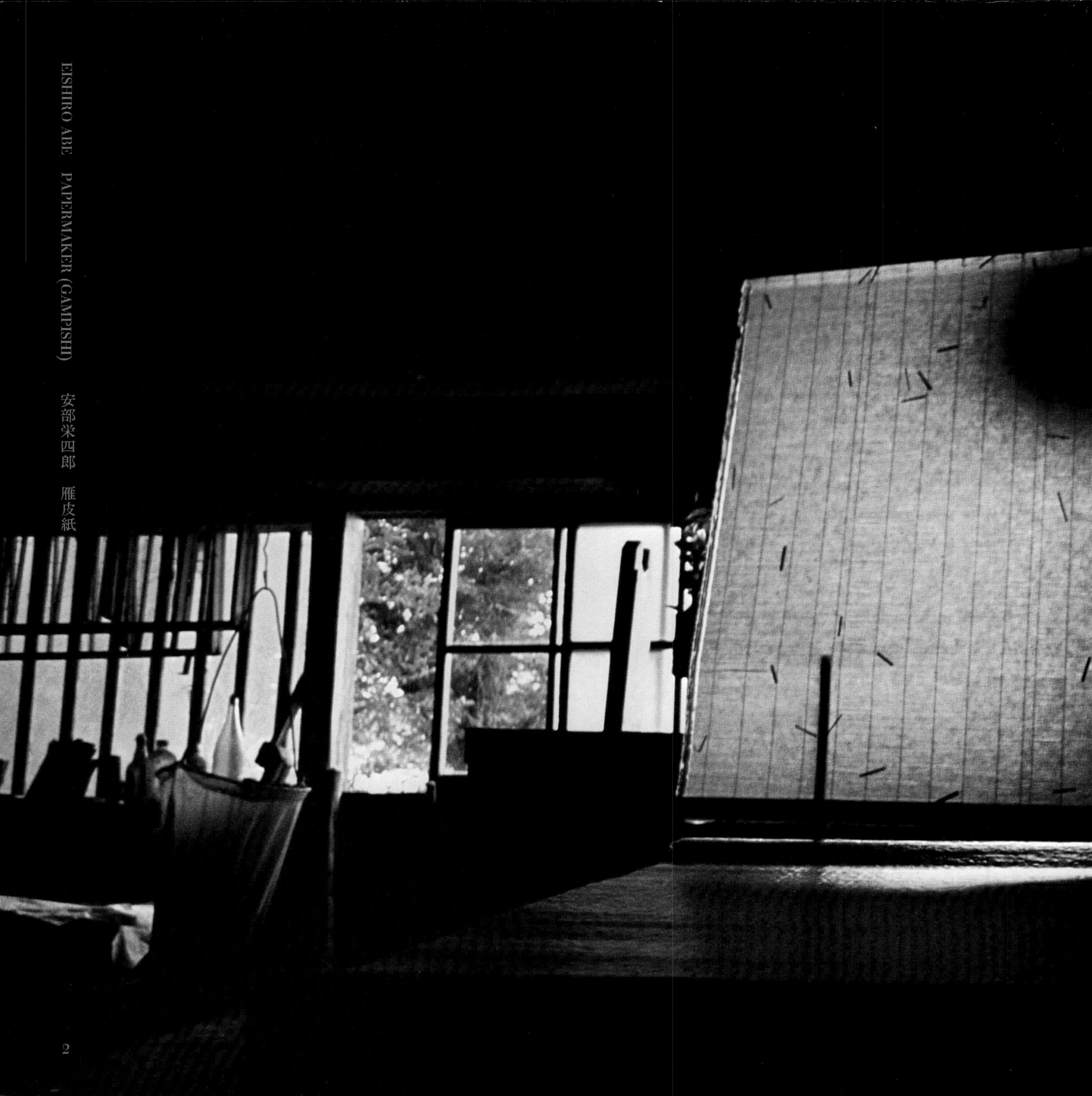

3

After steaming and the stripping of the outer bark, the inner bark is dried in the sun.

Steamer.

The bark is then washed in running water to soften and assist in whitening it.

Stripping the black bark.

4

An apprentice at work
over one of the wooden vats.
It takes atleast 2 years
practice to achieve an
even thickness of
fibres across the screen.

Although Abe prefers
the natural sunshine
drying method, he must
also use indoor steam
drying. The lady has
been working here for
30 years, says it is
a nice job in the winter.

6

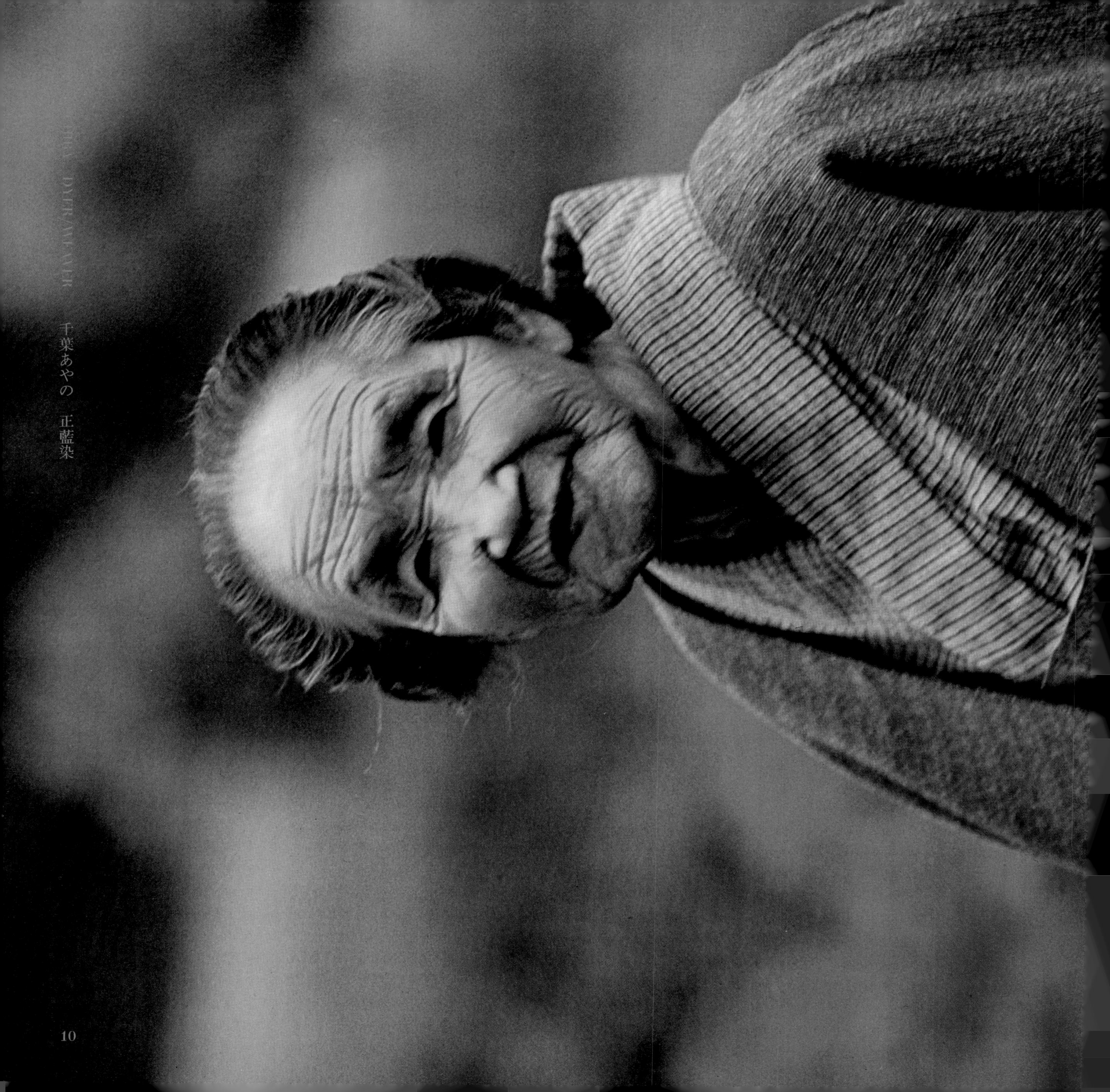

千葉あやの　正藍染

To soften the asa which grows behind her house, Mrs Chiba cooks it in salt water, then in the water poured off rice when being washed. This also bleaches it. Finally it has to be beaten against the floor to get it soft enough to spin.

To remove the nori (paste resist)
from the cloth, Mrs Chiba takes
the cloth to the river and the
fish nibble the nori off.
All the indigo dyed material
is washed there also, and
when dried, is absolutely fast.

Crumpling the leaves of ai — indigo,
before being left on rice-straw matting
to dry in the sun.

15

SHOJI HAMADA   POTTER (MINGEI)

浜田庄司　民芸陶器

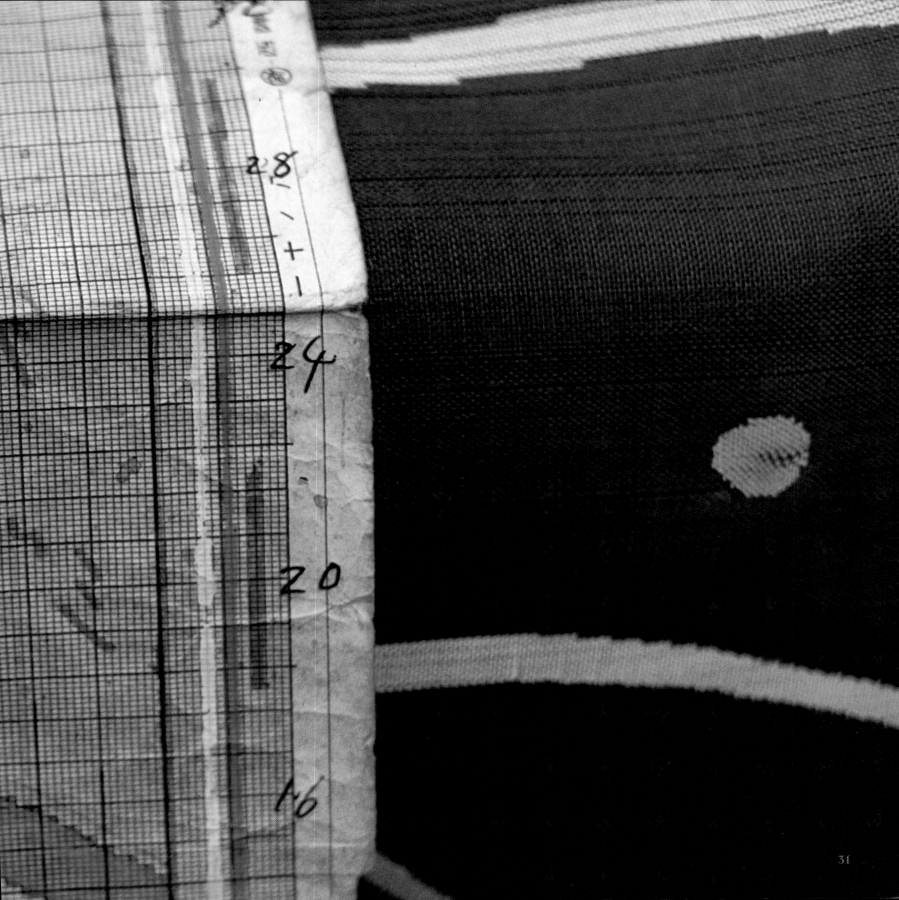

33

39

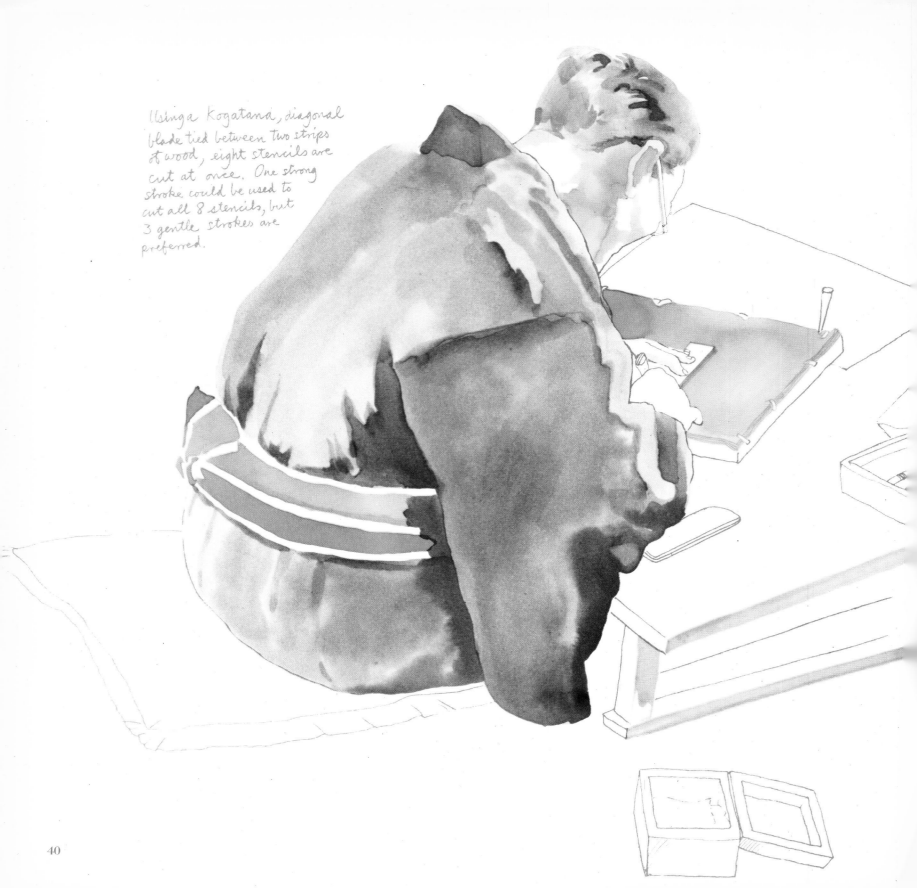

Using a Kogatana, diagonal blade tied between two strips of wood, eight stencils are cut at once. One strong stroke could be used to cut all 8 stencils, but 3 gentle strokes are preferred.

40

21 denier silk
is strung across
a wooden frame
edged with
wooden pegs.
The frame is placed
over another
frame on which
the bottom stencil
has been pasted.

Laying the top stencil over the
wet mesh and aligning it with
the bottom stencil. Sticky juice
is then brushed onto the top
stencil.

Using a needle-tipped stick to adjust
the silk mesh — some threads
are moved to add support to
delicate areas of the design.

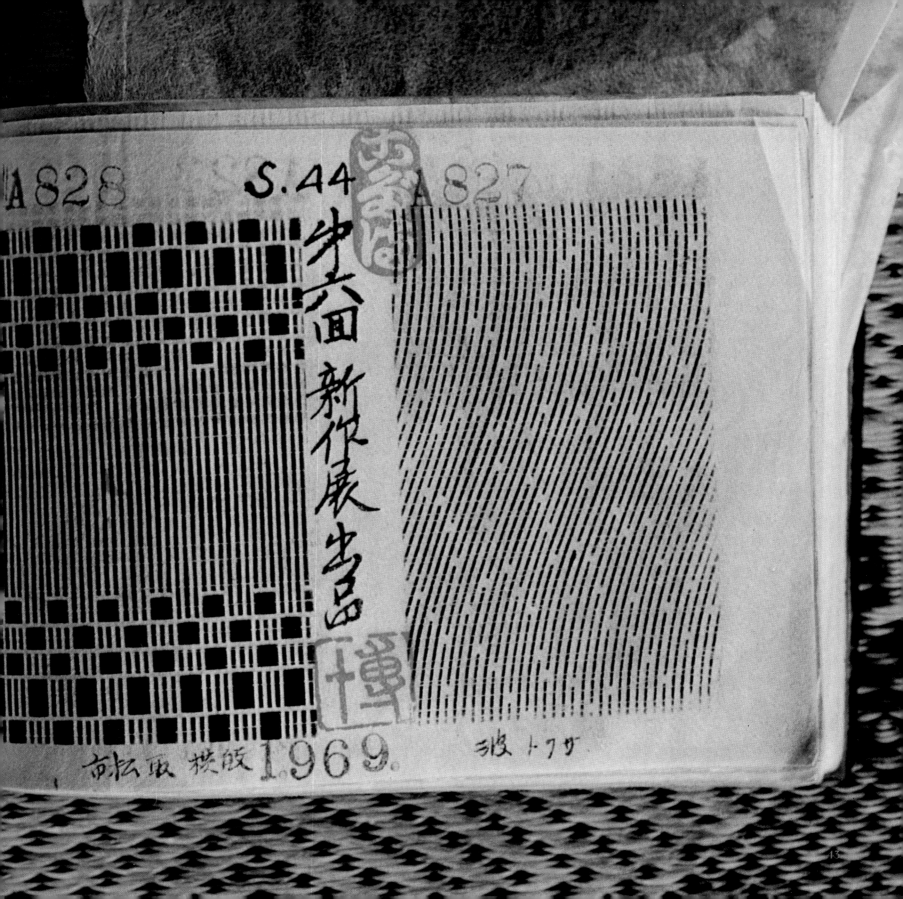

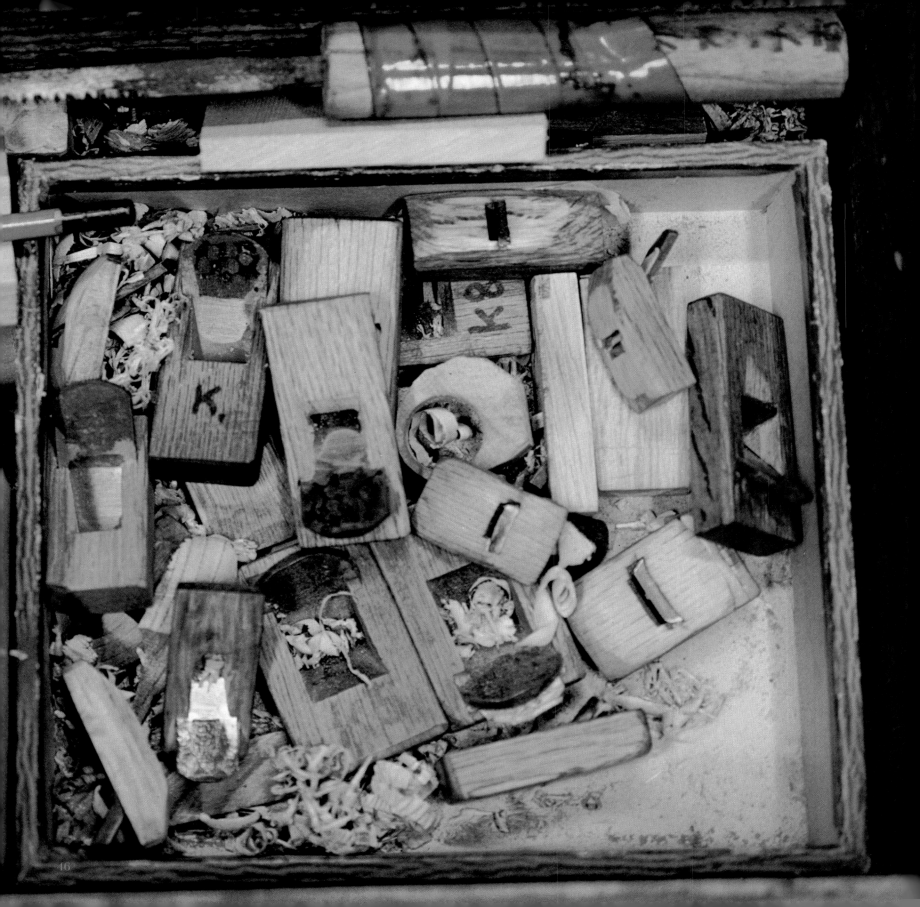

The small and literally spotless
workroom of Matsuda.
Triple sliding doors and window
panels keep out dust.
He sketches frequently in his
garden and many of his
designs are direct evidence
of this.

52

The tsu-tsu, a bamboo tube with silk
gauze across one end, is used to apply
powder of gold or silver onto wet lacquer.
Matsuda fingers tube like a small flute,
each finger providing a different texture.
Little finger makes finest.
Sometimes uses three fingers in
rythms and varies angle of tube.

54

三輪休
陶芸萩

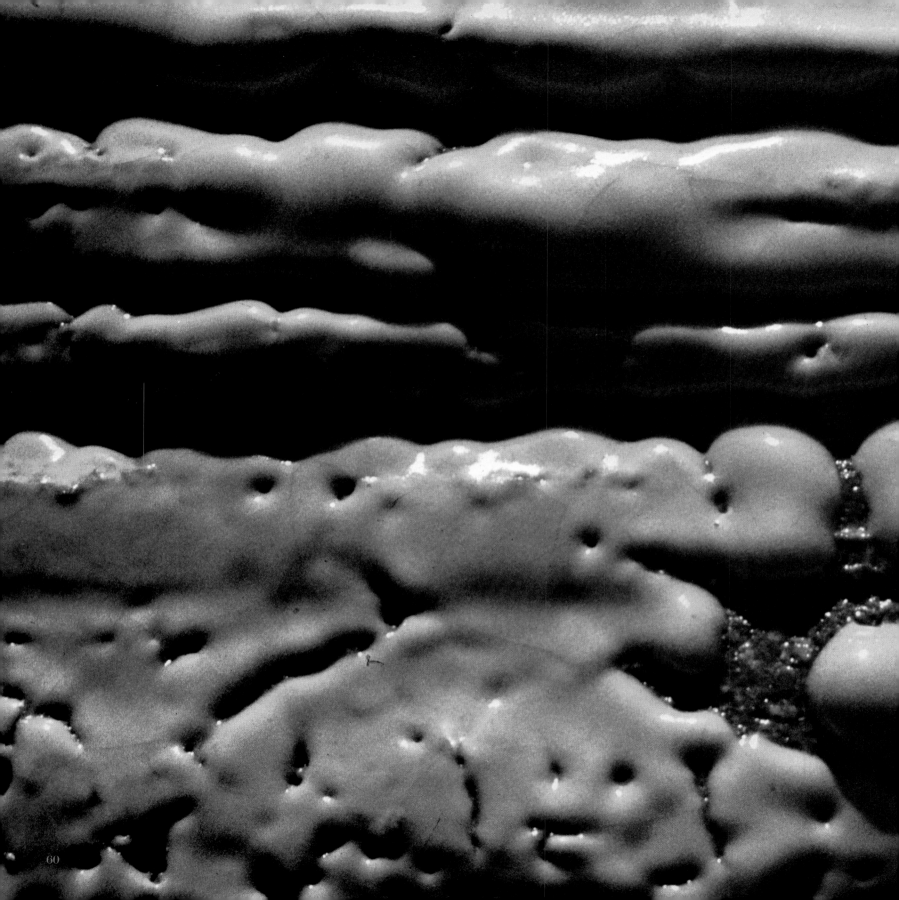

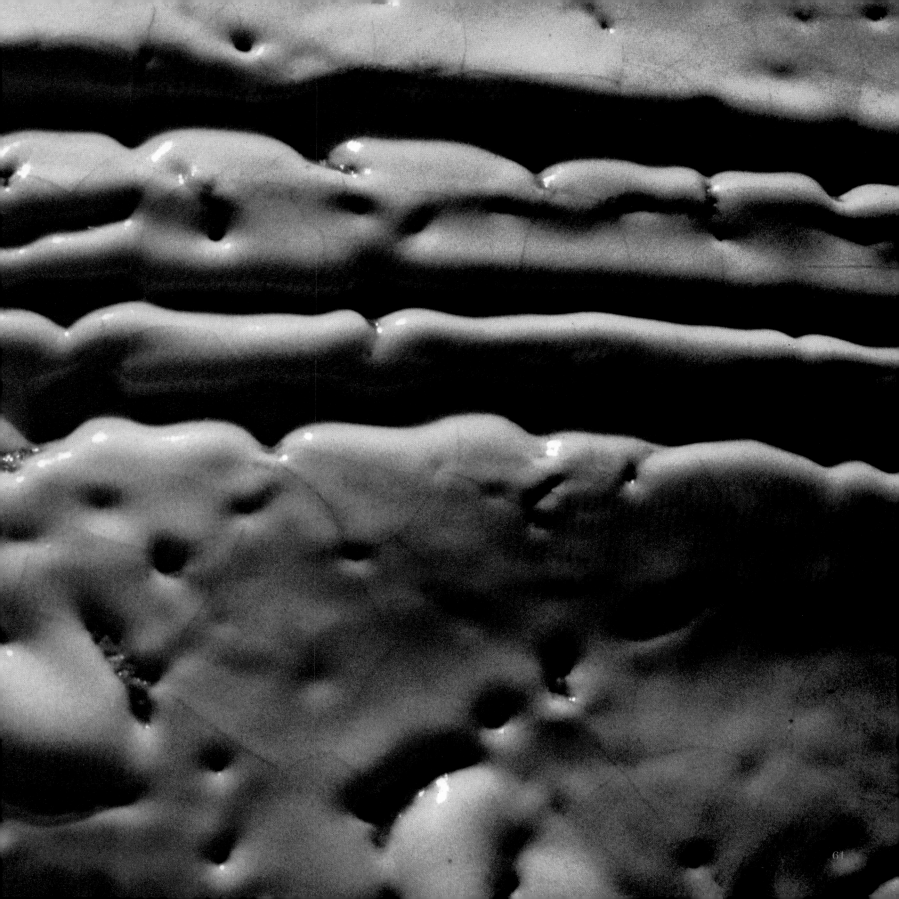

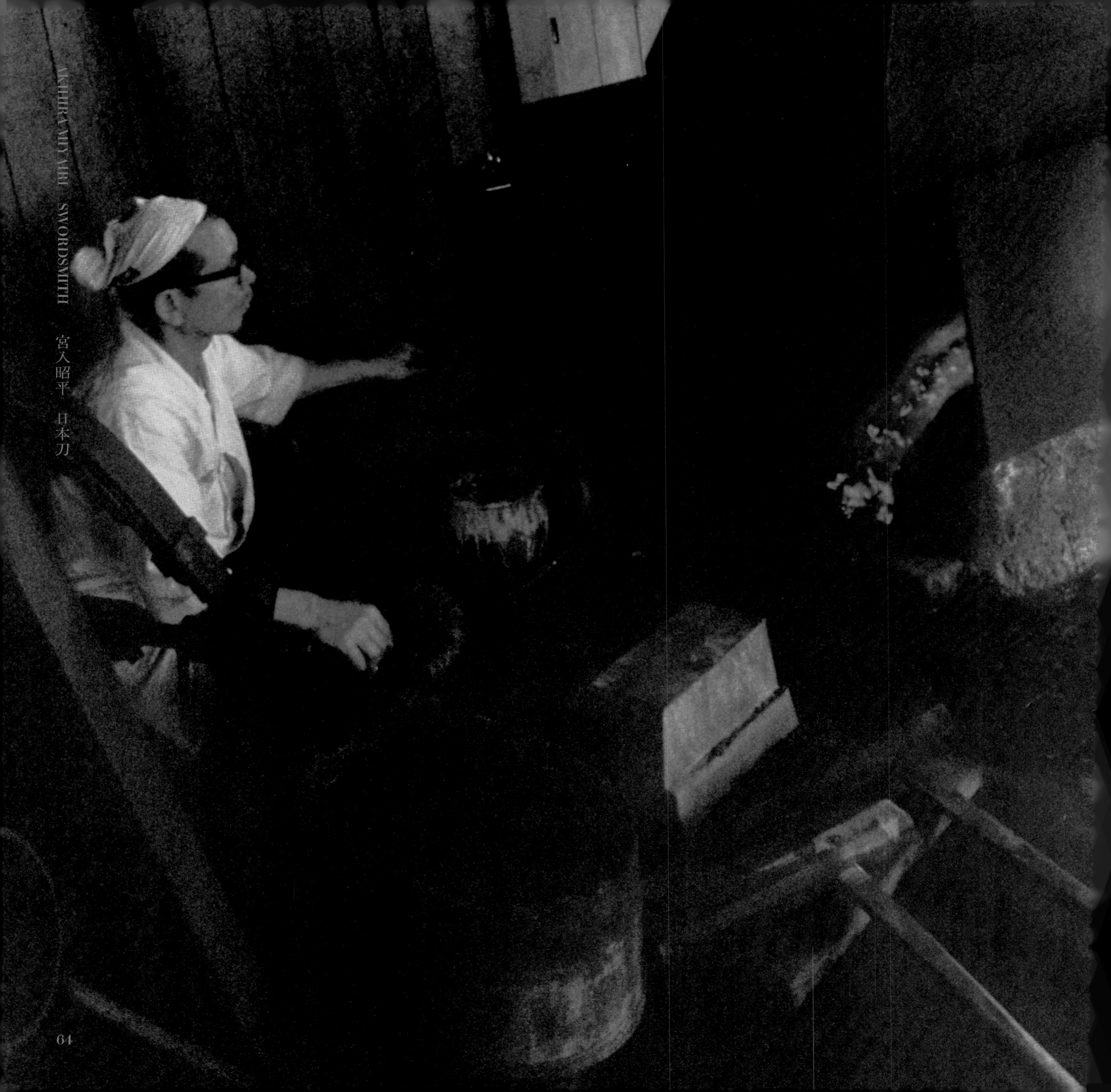

AKIHIRA MIYAIRI SWORDSMITH 宮入昭平 日本刀

charcoal store

smithy used by apprentices

After being heated for about 30 minutes, the molten metal is pounded with 25lb sledgehammers. Then, after sprinkling it with rice straw ashes and clay water, the small block of metal is placed back in the forge.

The heating and hammering process is repeated 7 or 8 times before the metal has been fused enough to start the folding

67

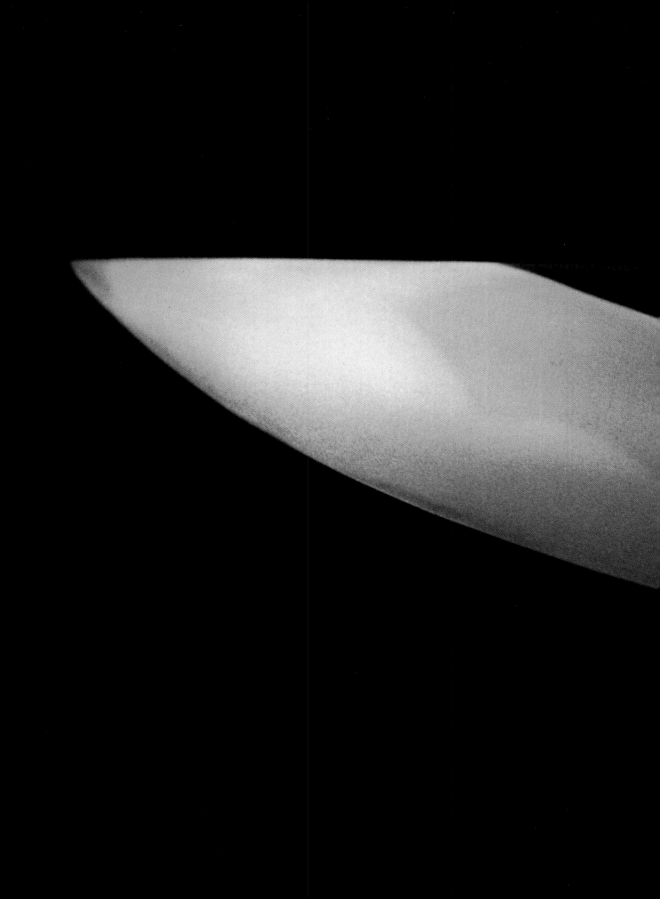

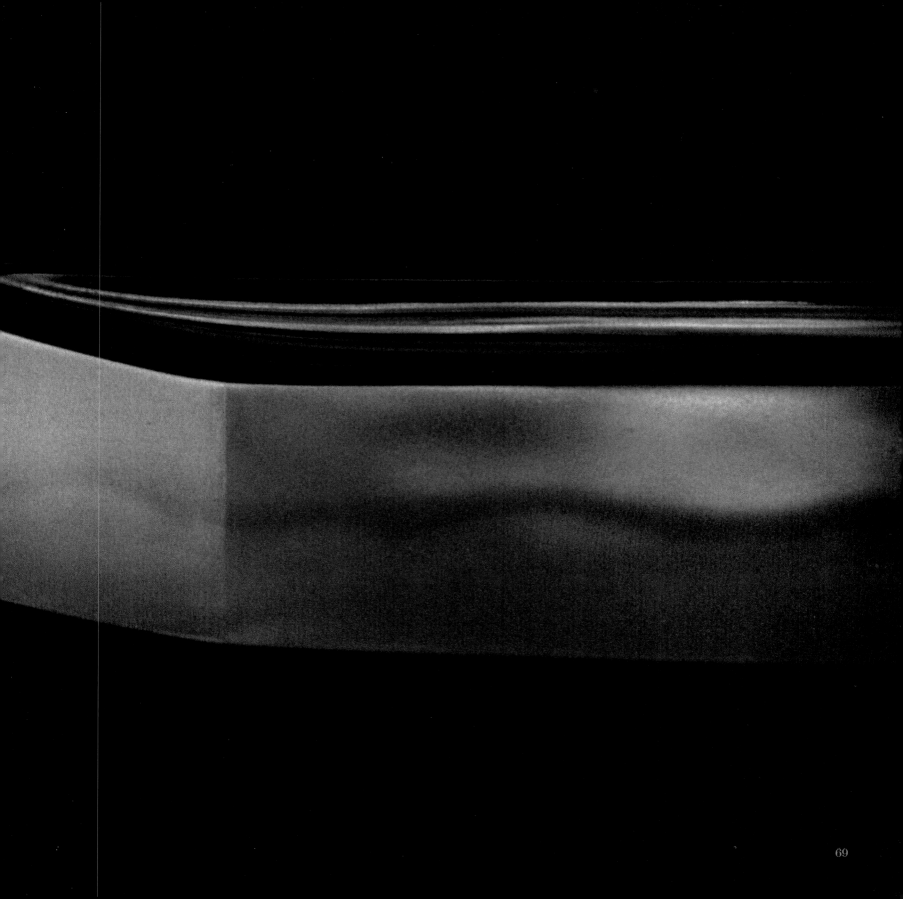

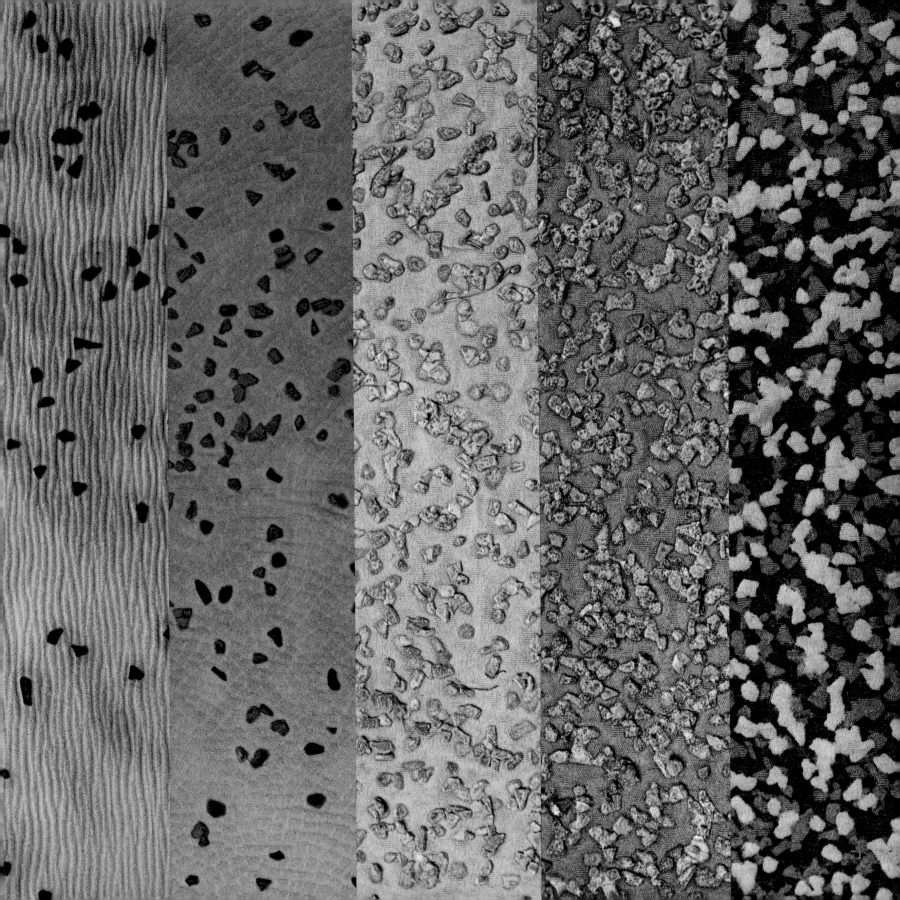

Maki-nori, a dry paste resist
is sprinkled on to wet cloth,
before it is brushed with dye.

72

A design is sketched
directly onto a Kimono
with a charcoal pencil

and then overpainted
with the juice of a wild
blue flower, the aobana,
which can later be
completely washed out
in water.

Removing excess
grains of resist,
one at a time,
until the desired
density is achieved.

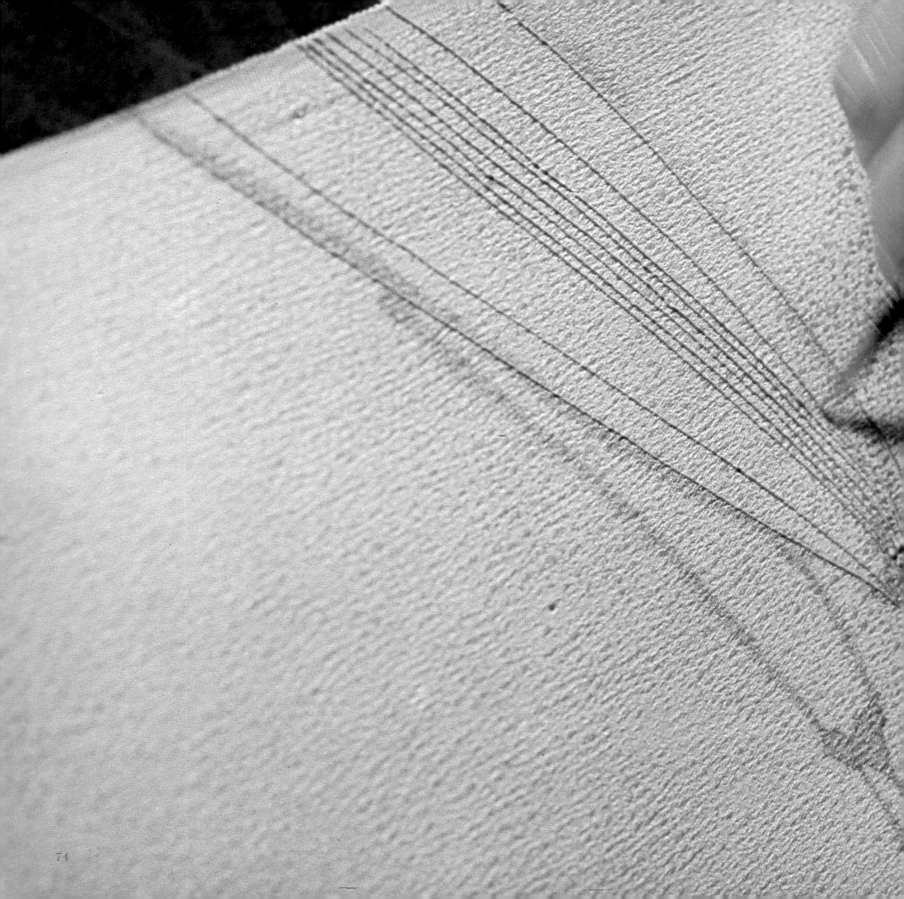

74

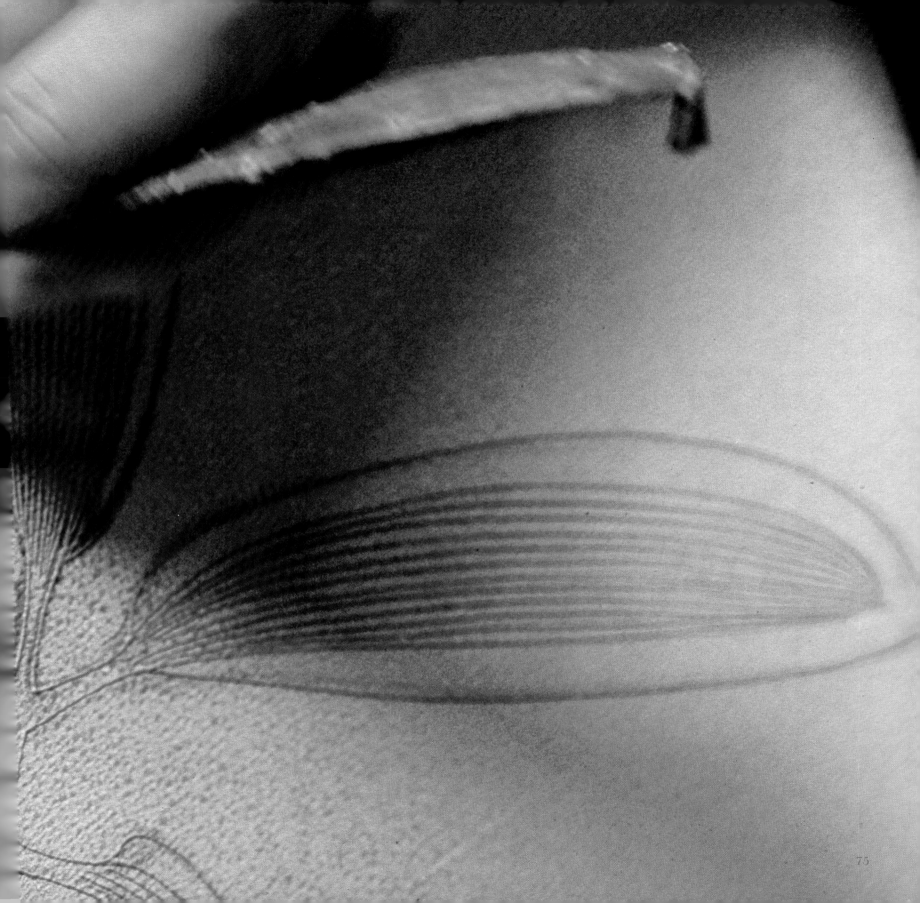

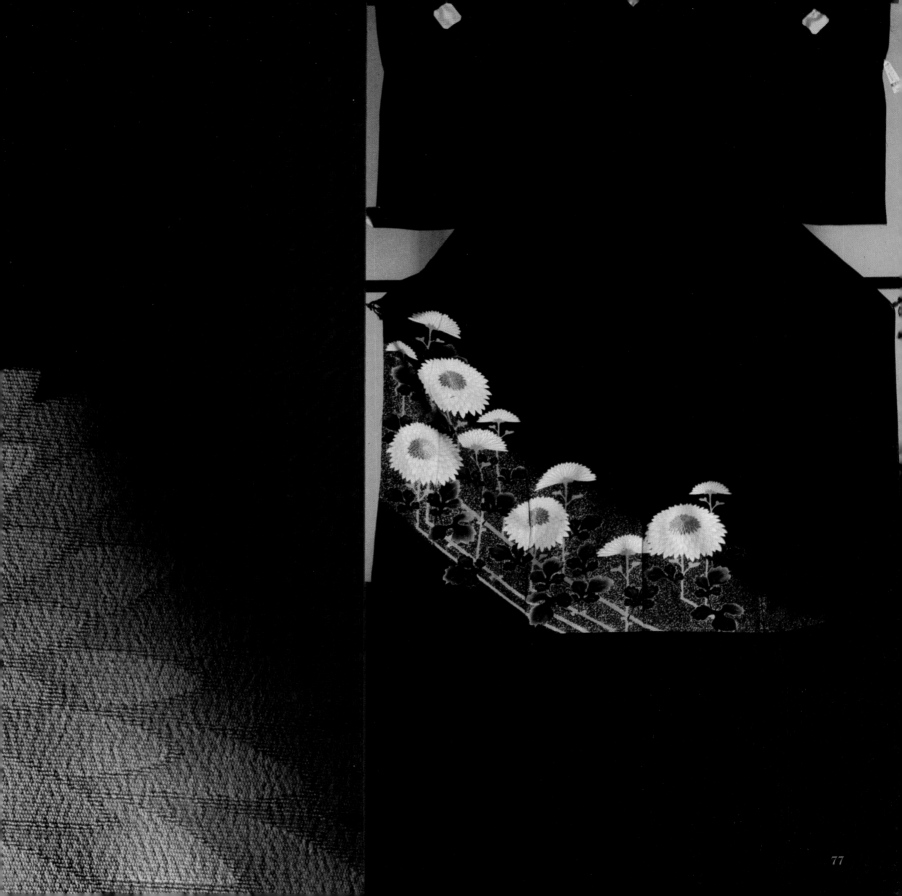

YOSHIMATSU NAMBU STENCIL CUTTER (ISE KATAGAMI DIE SINKER)

南部芳松　伊勢型紙突彫

KOTARO SHIMIZU STENCILER

清水幸太郎　長板中形

82

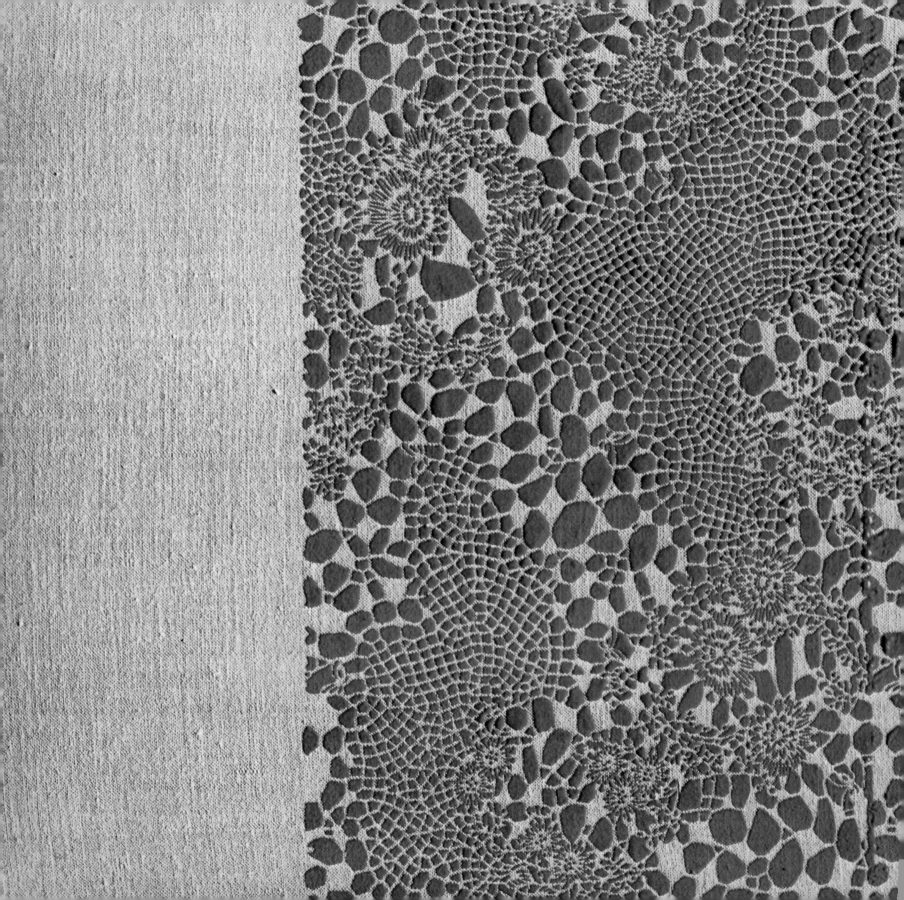

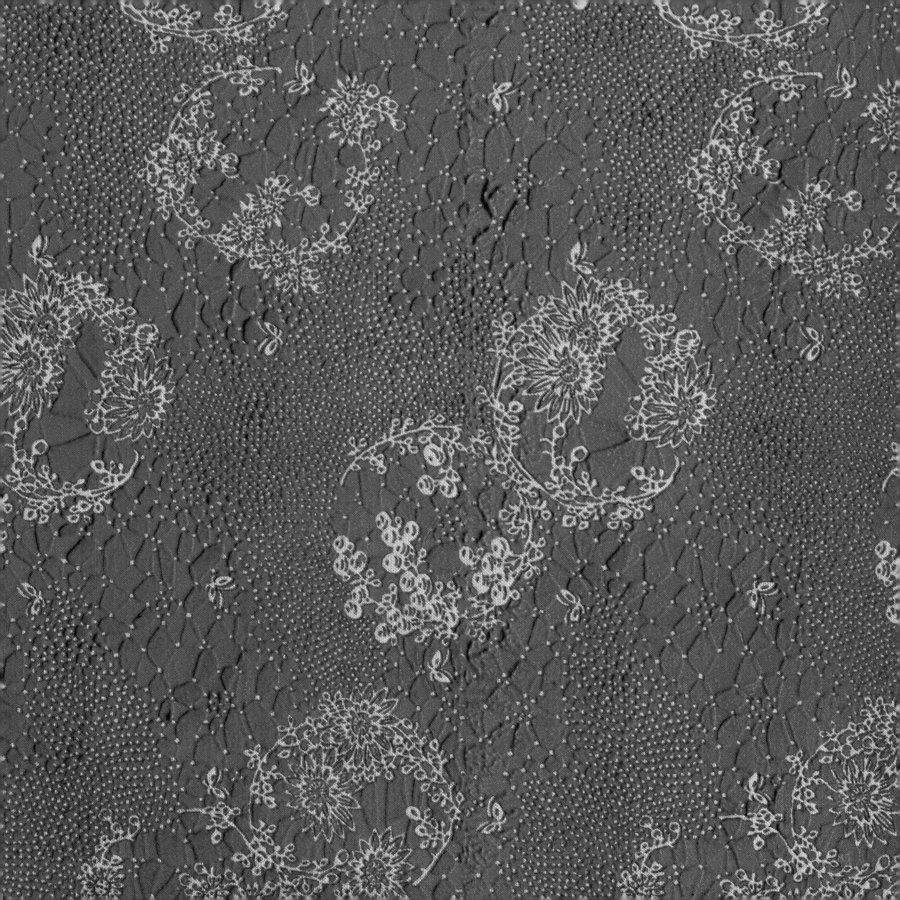

The lengths of fabric are hung across yard and painted twice with soya bean juice to make the resist fast.

Bamboo ribs are used to keep fabric taught and also make convenient handles during dying process.

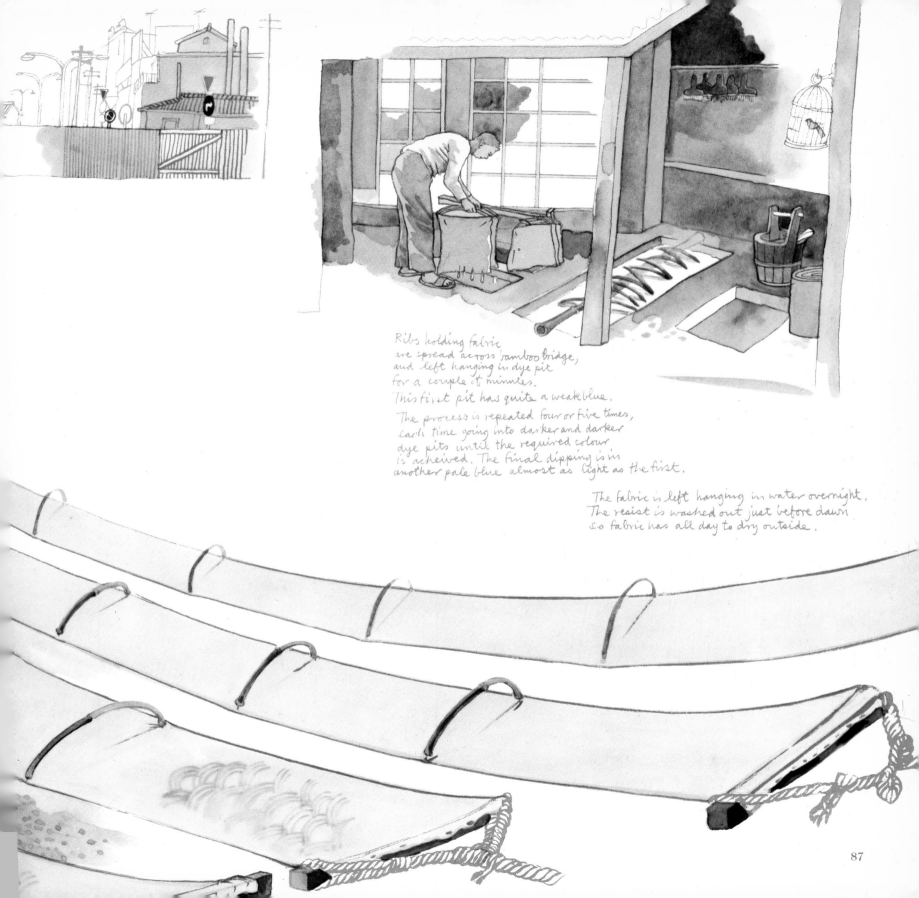

Ribs holding fabric
are spread across bamboo bridge,
and left hanging in dye pit
for a couple of minutes.
This first pit has quite a weak blue.

The process is repeated four or five times,
each time going into darker and darker
dye pits until the required colour
is acheived. The final dipping is in
another pale blue almost as light as the first.

The fabric is left hanging in water overnight.
The resist is washed out just before dawn
so fabric has all day to dry outside.

Index/Glossary

This Glossary is designed to clarify the text and does not repeat explanations. Terms used in one craft often have different meanings in other crafts, and various terms for the same tool or process may be used by different workers in the same craft.

decorative shapes and applied to a lacquered surface, 38

ichimai-zuki, stencil-cutting technique using a straight-bladed perforator, 30

Ido bowls, 41–42

Igarashi, Doho, 17th century Kanazawa lacquer artist, 5th master of Igarashi school of lacquerwork, 35

Ihara, Saikaku (1641–93), 47

Imbe, 17, 19

Imperial Regalia, 44

Imperial Repository, *see* Shoso-in

India, 7

indigo (*ai; Polygonium tinctorum*), 11, 13–16, 52–55; Pls. 14, 15, 17, 87–89

inlay, 33, 36–40

irori, open, sunken hearth used for heating and cooking, 15

Ise, 28–31, 50–52

    Grand Shrine(s) of, 28, 43–45

    -Kaido, 28

    katagami, paper stencils made in Ise area, 29–31, 50–52, 54; Pls. 38, 39, 78, 80–81

ito-ire (literally, "thread insertion"), technique of strengthening paper stencils by inserting a webbing of silk threads between the two sheets comprising a single stencil, 30; Pl. 41

Izumo, 11–13

Jacquard cards, perforated cards that control the harnesses of a loom, 26, 27

ji-gami, strong, white mulberry paper used to make stencils (term used before paper is coated with tannin and cured), 30

jigane (literally, "basic metal"), the iron used to make steel swords; smelted from ore, ferruginous sand, or pieces of iron of various qualities and strengths and forged into waferlike pieces, 43–45; Pls. 65–67

jihada, the area of the sword blade between the line (*hamon*) of the tempered edge (*yakiba*) and the ridge (*shinogi*), 45

Jimmu, Emperor (660–585 B.C.), legendary first emperor of Japan, 44

Jomon period (ca. 10,000–200 B.C.), Japan's Neolithic period, named after characteristic cord-marked pottery, 38

Kaga, 46

kaki-shibu, see persimmon tannin

Kamakura period (1185–1333), period of first shogunate, 18, 43, 44, 58

Kamo River, 48, 54

Kanazawa, 37

kanoko (literally, "fawn"), used to describe the ocellus or eye pattern produced by tie-dyeing and imitated in stencilling and dyeing, 52

Kanto earthquake, 54

Kara-ori (literally, "Chinese weave"), weaving technique designed to imitate embroidery; areas of colored threads remain loose on the textile surface and give the effect of embroidered stitches. *Kara-ori* brocades are used mostly for priest robes and Noh costumes for female roles; also a generic term for Noh costumes for female roles, 26; Pl. 34–35

katagami, paper stencils, 28–31, 50–53

Katsura Imperial Villa, 12

kawagane (literally, "skin metal"), the hard steel used for the surface of a sword, folded or wrapped over the core of softer and more flexible steel (*shingane*), 45

Kawai, Kanjiro, 12, 22, 35

Kenzan, *see* Ogata, Kenzan

keshi-gata (literally, "blotting-out stencil"), secondary stencil of a pair of stencils used to create intricate designs; approximately 30 percent of the pattern is cut on the *keshi-gata*, 55; Pl. 85, see also *omo-gata*

keta, wooden frame or mold used to hold the bamboo screen on which paper is laid, 13; Pl. 6

keyaki, zelkova wood, 6, 32–35; Pl. 47

Kii (Peninsula), 29

kiji, core, body, or base for lacquerwork, 39

kilns, 18, 19, 21, 23, 41, 42; Pl. 24

kimono(s), 29, 46–55; Pls. 70, 76–77

kin-ji, polished gold lacquer ground, 40

kinran (literally, "gold-patterned textile or brocade"), a plain-weave silk with a weft pattern created with paper-backed gold leaf or gold-covered paper thread, 26, 27

kiri, paulownia wood (Chinese character differs from *kiri* below), 33, 34

kiri, awllike stencil-cutting tool with a tiny

crescent-shaped blade that is used to make fine perforations with a punching and rotating motion, 29, 30

kiri-bori, stencil-cutting technique using a *kiri* to make designs composed of fine perforations, 29–31

Kitano tea party, 18

Kizaemon, 42

Ko-Bizen (literally, "old Bizen"), a school of early swordmaking (ca. 950–1200), 44

Kobori Enshu (d.1647), 17th century tea master, 42

Koetsu, 22, 37, 42

kogatana (literally, "small sword or blade"), term used to refer to various knives and cutting tools; here, specifically, wood-hafted blades for cutting paper stencils, 30, 51; Pl. 40

kokoro, heart, heart and mind, spirit, 49

kokuso, wet, plasterlike mixture of liquid lacquer, rice paste, and pounded hemp used as primer for wooden cores of articles to be lacquered, 39

komon (literally, "small pattern"), fine design achieved by stencil-resist dyeing, 29

Konjikido, main hall of Chusonji temple in Hiraizumi, 38

Koraizaemon, Japanese name of Li Kyong, 16th century Korean potter, 41

Korea, 6, 10, 14, 18, 22, 25, 33, 37, 40–42, 58–59

Korin, *see* Ogata, Korin

kozo (*Broussonetia papyrifera*), paper mulberry shrub; also the paper made from this material, 10–13, *see also* mulberry, paper

kunenjo, smokehouse in which mulberry paper impregnated with persimmon tannin is cured and colored by smoke produced by burning sawdust, 51

Kurikoma, 14

kuro-chiku (*Phyllostachys nigra*), black bamboo, 57

kuwa, silk mulberry plant, the leaves of which are used to feed silkworms and the bark of which may be used for paper, basketry, and weaving, 13

Kyoto, 11, 12, 14, 22, 24, 26, 28, 32, 44, 46–49, 57

Kyushu, 57

measuring between 11 to 12 meters long and 30 to 40 centimeters wide, 15

T'ang dynasty (618–907), 25

Tange, Kenzo, 12

Tango, 47

tanto, a straight-bladed dirk, usually under 35 centimeters long, 45

Taut, Bruno, 12

Tawaraya, 24–26

tea ceremony (*cha-no-yu* or *chado*), 11, 12, 18–26, 33, 41–42, 58

Temmu, Emperor (ruled 673–686), 33

Thailand, 40

Three Sacred Treasures, 44

togi-dashi (literally, "brought out by polishing-down or burnishing"), technique of lacquer decoration in which a design is painted on a prepared lacquer ground, then sprinkled with metallic dusts or grains (usually gold) or powdered pigments; the entire surface of the object is then given a thick coat of opaque colored lacquer and scoured with polishing stones or charcoal to reveal the gold or colored design, 37, 39, see also *maki-e*

Tokaido, 28

tokkuri, saké bottle, usually ceramic, 19

Tokoname, 18

Tokugawa shogunate (1615–1868), government by military rulers of the Tokugawa line; Ieyasu Tokugawa (1542–1616) defeated Hideyoshi and established the shogunate with Edo as the capital, 12, 29, *see also* Edo period

tokusa, a reedlike grass, rush, 47

Tokyo, 29, 60

Tomimoto, Kenkichi, 22, 35

tororo aoi, a tuber similar to taro; used for its starch, 11, 13

Toyotomi, Hideyoshi (1536–98), military ruler and patron of the arts, 18, 26, 29, 41, 42

trailing, glaze, 22

Ts'ai Lun, 11

tsubo, jar or storage vessel, usually ceramic, 19

tsuge, boxwood, 34

tsuki-bori, stencil cutting technique in which the *hori-kogatana* is used, 29, 52, see *hori-kogatana*

tsutsu, tube of bamboo or crane feather shaft used to sprinkle gold, silver, and shell dust in lacquerwork, 39; Pls. 53–55

tsutsugami, metal-tipped mulberry paper funnel used for squeezing paste resist onto kimono material; paper is waterproofed with persimmon tannin, 47; Pls. 74–75

Tsutsumi-ga-ura (literally, "Bay of the Drum"), 50–51

tsuzure-ori (literally, "vine weaving"), a tapestry weave, 25

urushi, lacquer, q.v.

Vietnam, 40

wabi, 26, 27

washi, traditional Japanese paper, made of tree or vegetable fibers, 11–22, 44

wax resist, 21

weaving, 14–16, 25–26; Pls. 30–35

wheel, potter's, 17–19, 21, 42

White Heron Castle, 44

woodblock prints, 12

wool, 14, 16

yakiba, tempered edge of a sword, 45

yakogai, a mollusk of *Turbo* genus, having a nacrous inside shell used for inlay, 33, 38

Yakumo, 8

Yamashiro smiths, swordsmiths of the Yamashiro school in Yamashiro Province (Kyoto area); active late 10th to early 15th century, 44

yama-zakura, wild cherry tree, 34

Yanagi, Soetsu, 7, 22, 35

Yayoi period (ca. 200 B.C. – A.D. 200), period that saw the introduction of potter's wheel and rice agriculture from the continent, 14, 18

Yi dynasty (1392–1910), 22

Yüan dynasty (1279–1368), 26

yugen, 26

yukata, unlined cotton kimono, usually patterned in indigo blue and white, 52, 53–55; Pls. 88–89

yuzen, 46–49

zangurishita, a pleasantly rough texture, 18

Zen, 6, 18, 25, 57, 59